Photoshop® CS KillerTips

PHOTOSHOP® CS KILLER TIPS

The Photoshop® CS
Killer Tips Team

TECHNICAL EDITOR
Chris Main

COPY EDITOR
Barbara Thompson

PRODUCTION EDITOR
Kim Gabriel

PRODUCTION
Dave Damstra
Dave Korman

PROOFREADER
Daphne Durkee

COVER DESIGN AND
CREATIVE CONCEPTS
Felix Nelson

SITE DESIGN
Stacy Behan

PUBLISHED BY
New Riders Publishing / Peachpit Press

Copyright © 2004 by Scott Kelby

FIRST EDITION: February 2004

Composed in Myriad and Minion by NAPP Publishing

Trademarks

Warning and Disclaimer

ISBN 0-7357-1356-1

9 8 7 6 5 4 3 2

Printed and bound in the United States of America

To my Dad,

Jerry Kelby,

for being

the father

everyone

wishes

they had

—SCOTT KELBY

To Patty,

Alex, Chris,

and Earl.

They truly are

my strength

and inspiration

—FELIX NELSON

ACKNOWLEDGMENTS

As I'm writing this acknowledgment, I'm finally learning what the downside of being a coauthor is: You only get half as much space to thank all of the great people without whom you couldn't do any of this.

First, I want to thank my incredible wife, Kalebra. I don't know what she puts in her morning coffee, but it must be working. Every year she gets more amazing, more beautiful, more hilarious, more savvy, and more just plain wonderful. She's my best friend, confidante, advice desk, gourmet chef, favorite artist, and the ultimate business partner. Best of all, she's a world-class mom, and it's an absolute joy seeing her special gifts reflected in our son Jordan. He has no idea how blessed and supremely lucky we both are to have her.

I want to thank my coauthor, Felix Nelson, for agreeing to do this book with me. He's an amazing person—a great artist, with seemingly limitless enthusiasm and energy that has him perpetually in a good mood seven days a week.

His combination of talent, business savvy, and humor make him an absolute pleasure to work with, and I continue to learn more from him every day. I want to thank my Tech Editor Chris Main and Production Editor Kim Gabriel for once again bringing the whole project together and kicking butt every step of the way. Also thanks to Barbara Thompson for all her hard work and dedication to this project, and to Dave Korman and Daphne Durkee.

I want to thank the Photoshop experts from whom I've learned so much over the years, including Julieanne Kost, Ben Willmore, Russell Preston Brown, Doug Gornick, Deke McClelland, Jack Davis, and Robb Kerr. I also want to thank my good friends and business partners, Jim Workman and Jean A. Kendra, my brother Jeff for everything he does and for being such an important part of my life. I want to thank everyone at KW Media Group—they excel at the whole "David and Goliath" thing. An extra special thanks to Kathy Siler for the hundreds of things she does for me that make my life and my work so much easier.

Thanks to Steve Weiss and Nancy Ruenzel at Peachpit for their commitment to excellence, and for the honor of letting me be one of their "Voices That Matter," and to Jeff Schultz for bringing us all together in the first place.

And most importantly, an extra special thanks to God and his son Jesus Christ for always hearing my prayers, for always being there when I need Him, and for blessing me with a life I truly love, and a warm loving family to share it with.

—*SCOTT KELBY*

First, I'd like to thank my wife, Patty, who is the kindest, most understanding and caring person on the face of the planet. Her positive outlook on life, no matter how chaotic the world is around her, is remarkable. A smile from her face can light up an entire room. Then there are my three sons, Earl, Chris, and Alex. Earl is the ultimate in cool. Nothing ever ruffles his feathers. To watch an adorable, curly-headed little boy grow up into such a wonderful young man has been my greatest source of pride. And Chris "the studier" is the hardest-working, nose-to-the-grindstone person you'd ever want to meet. His drive and determination astonishes me. He's just a fantastic kid. Then there's little Alex. It's absolutely amazing how this little person affects my life. No matter how bad or how stressful the day has been, a hug from those tiny little arms and an "I love you Daddy" from those big brown eyes just melt my heart. He makes me realize things are never quite as bad as they appear.

My involvement in this book would not have been possible without the guidance and tutelage of Scott Kelby. He is without a doubt the most energetic, ambitious, and entertaining person I've ever met. His motor just never stops running. I can't begin to tell you how much he's influenced my life. He's a great mentor and a wonderful human being. I also have to thank the partners of KW Media Group (Jim Workman, Jean Kendra, and Kalebra Kelby) for the opportunities they've given me. When it comes to hard work and dedication, they're right up there with Scott. They're an amazing group, and I'm a better person for knowing them.

Thanks to Dave Moser and Kim Gabriel who, come hell or high water, make sure the trains run on time. If it weren't for their efforts, this book might never had made it to the presses. Of course, I can't forget about Dave "Dude" Korman and "Super Dave" Damstra, who do the work of ten ordinary designers. They flat out kick butt. Chris Main and Barbara Thompson could proofread an entire set of encyclopedias in an afternoon, and still have time for beer and a game of darts. I couldn't make it through the workday without them. Thanks to everyone at KW Media group, working behind the scenes, from the mailroom to customer service, who make us all look good. And a special thanks to "Rockin" Ronni, Jeff, Stacy, Kevin, and Daphne. They should all be up for sainthood just for putting up with me on a daily basis.

—*FELIX NELSON*

Scott Kelby

Scott is Editor-in-Chief and co-founder of *Photoshop User* magazine, Editor-in-Chief of Nikon's *Capture User* magazine, and Editor-in-Chief of *Mac Design Magazine*. He is President of the National Association of Photoshop Professionals (NAPP), the trade association for Adobe® Photoshop® users, and he's President of KW Media Group, Inc., a Florida-based software education and publishing firm.

Scott is author of the best-selling books *Photoshop CS Down & Dirty Tricks* and *The Photoshop CS Book for Digital Photographers,* and he's creator and series Editor for the Killer Tips series from New Riders Publishing. Scott has authored two best-selling Macintosh books: *Mac OS X Jaguar Killer Tips* and the award-winning *Macintosh: The Naked Truth,* both also from New Riders, and the new *Mac OS X Conversion Kit: 9 to 10 side by side* from Peachpit Press.

Scott introduced his first software title in 2003 called "Kelby's Notes for Adobe Photoshop" which adds the answers to the 100 most-asked Photoshop questions, accessed from directly within Photoshop.

Scott is Training Director for the Adobe Photoshop Seminar Tour, Conference Technical Chair for the PhotoshopWorld Conference & Expo, and he is a speaker at graphics trade shows and events around the world. He is also featured in a series of Adobe Photoshop training videos and DVDs and has been training Adobe Photoshop users since 1993.

For more background info on Scott, visit www.scottkelby.com.

Felix Nelson

Felix is the Creative Director of *Photoshop User* and *Capture User* magazines and the Senior Art Director for the National Association of Photoshop Professionals. Felix is also the Art Director for *Mac Design Magazine*.

Felix is a contributing author to the book *Photoshop Effects Magic* from New Riders Publishing and served as technical consultant for the book *Adobe Photoshop Down & Dirty Tricks*. He is also featured in a new Photoshop training video—*Photoshop Photorealistic Techniques.*

He's a traditional illustrator who took a "digital u-turn" in 1988 when he was first introduced to a Mac IIcx. His design work and digital illustrations have been featured on NBA-, NFL-, and MLB-licensed sports apparel and have appeared in several national publications.

Felix is a guest speaker at the Adobe Photoshop Seminar Tour and is a part of the PhotoshopWorld Instructor "Dream Team."

Felix lives in Spring Hill, Florida, with his wife Patty and sons Alex, Chris, and Earl.

CHAPTER 1   1

Life in the Fast Lane
Production Tips

Making the Preview Palette Bigger   2
Saving File Browser Setups   2
Setting Defaults in the Filter Gallery   3
Rearranging Your Brushes   3
Creating Your Own Custom New Document Presets   4
Find the Center of Any Document   4
No More Jaggy Lasso Tool Selections   5
The Menu to Full Screen Mode   6
Experimenting with Zoom   6
Open up Some Screen Real Estate   7
Let Photoshop Do the Work in Curves   8
Want a Finer Grid? You Got It!   8
You Don't Need the Brushes Palette
  to Change Brush Size   9
Rotate to Any Angle the Fast Way   9
Removing Points from the Polygonal Lasso   10
Getting to the Right Palette Just Got Easier   10
Opening an Image and Closing the File Browser   11
Opening Multiple Images and Closing the Browser   11
Get Rid of Unwanted Brushes   12
Navigating the Brush Picker Like a Pro   12
Get More Control over Your Paint Strokes   13
Speed Tip to Rotate Through Open Images   13
Instantly Find the Center of Any Object   14
Making Your Guide Flip   14
Creating Temporary Brushes   15
Reusing Your Last Curve Setting   15
Bringing Back Those Cropped-Away Areas   16
Fix Those Stray Pixels Fast!   16
Getting More Control over the Magic Wand   17
Making the Color Palette Work Twice as Hard   17
Photoshop Remembers the Last Size You Input   18
Seeing Your Curves up Close   18
Use Your Last Settings and Save Time   19
Hit Those Channels Fast   19
How to Get an Undo After You've Closed
  the Document   20
Using the Pen? Stay Away from the Toolbox   20
Put Your Gradient Picker at Your Fingertips   21
Don't Click in That Field!   21
Out of Memory? Try This First   22
How to "Unerase"   22
Let Photoshop Straighten Your Crooked Scans   23
Copy One Layer, or Copy 'Em All   23
Stuck in a Field? Here's How to Escape   24

TABLE OF CONTENTS

Don't Cancel; Reset and Save Time	24
Time for Some Pantone Convenience	25
How to Hide the Path around Your Shape	25
Zooming in the Filter Gallery	26
See Every Tweak with Bigger Filter Gallery Previews	26
Showing One Effect in the Filter Gallery	27
Use the Move Tool Anytime	27
Filter Gallery Zoom Quick Tip	28
Trashing Filter Gallery Filters the Fast Way	28
Saving Your Favorite Folders in the File Browser	29
Nesting Your File Browser Palettes	29
Brushes Right Where You Want 'Em	30

CHAPTER 2	33
Born to Run	
Essential Tips You've Got to Know	

The Hidden Measurement Pop-Down Menu	34
Batch Renaming Made More Usable	34
Changing Metadata Font Sizes	35
Getting a Fresh Histogram in One Click	35
Using the Lasso Tool? Keep It Straight	36
Skip the Zoom Tool	36
Can't Remember Selection Shortcuts? Look at the Cursor	37
Snap Your Palettes to Order	37
Your Selections Aren't Stuck—Move 'Em!	38
One-Button Refresh for the File Browser	38
Get Rid of the Annoying Checkerboard Pattern	39
Understanding the Giant Mondo-Big Brushes Palette	39
How to Tame the Select Similar Command	40
Run That Filter One More Time	40
Don't Let the Browser Preview Fool You	41
Want the Default Colors? Just "D-Do" It	41
Scrubby Slider Shift-Click Trick	42
Saving Time in the Fill Dialog	42
Why the File Browser Won't Dock	43
Escape from the Crop Tool (or Die!)	43
Getting the Startup Window Back	44
Getting Your Warnings Back (Resetting All Dialogs)	44
How to See Your Vector EPS Files in the File Browser	45
The Smaller Toolbox Trick	45
Brushes Palette: That's Not a Header, It's a Button	46
Dangerous Intersection?	46
Nudging Power	47
Make That Options Bar Float—Float???	47
Where's the 3D Transform Filter?	48
The Fate of Clipping Groups	48
Supersize It	49

Lock Those Pixels and Fill 49
Steal Color from Anywhere 50
Ask Photoshop to Remember More 50
The Mondo-Cool Batch Ranking Secret Shortcut 51
Shrink Those Palettes Down to Size 51
Stop the Warnings from Your Digital Camera Images 52
Creating the Über Palette 52
Killing Layers with No Mercy 53
Tired of Pressing the Shift Key to Rotate
 through Tools? 53
Fix Those Tool Settings Fast 54
Bring Order Back to Your World 54
The Undocumented Fill Shortcut 55
Deselected and Forgot to Save? Don't Sweat It 55
Super-Fast Inches to Pixels 56
Lightning-Fast Feather 56
Boss Around Your Color Swatches 57
Zoomed In? Don't Use the Scroll Bars 57
Let Photoshop Do the Math When Copying/Pasting 58
Instant Selection from Any Path 58
Maximum File Browser Hidden Shortcut 59
Canvas Color Quick Change 59
Save Clicks When You Close 60
Been Binging on RAM? Maybe It's Time to Purge! 60
Reaching the Free Transform Handles 61
Transforming and Copying at the Same Time 61

CHAPTER 3 63
Greased Lightnin'
Way Cool Tips
The Trick to Tricky Extractions 64
Live Patching Preview 64
Zooming All Your Tiled Images at Once 65
Finding the Photographic Brush Tips 65
How to Duplicate a Color Stop 66
Removing Edge Fringe When Collaging 66
Cracking the Easter Egg Mystery 67
Supercharge Your Filter Effects 67
Undo on a Slider? 68
Getting to the Folder of Photos You Want—Fast! 68
Two Files Are Better Than One 69
Resizing Paths the Easy Way 69
The Gaussian Blur Keyboard Shortcut 70
The Advantage of Photo Filter Adjustment Layers 70
Where to Set Custom View Sizes 71
Moving Your Image in Full Screen Mode 71
Don't Rank It—Flag It 72
Photo-Retouching Safety Tip 72

TABLE OF CONTENTS

Photoshop's Hidden Step and Repeat	73
Pausing for a Brush Preview	73
The Undocumented Airbrush Toggle Trick	74
Give Most Anything a Keyboard Shortcut	74
No More Unlocking a Background Copy	75
Swapping Crop Fields	75
Let Those Windows Breathe!	76
The Multiple Undo Shortcut	76
Want Arrowheads? Photoshop Can Add Them for You!	77
Getting to the Free Transform Tool's Pop-Up List	77
Dragging and Dropping Where You Want	78
Custom Brushes Don't Have to Be Square Anymore	78
Feather a Selection without the Guessing Game	79
Creating a Flattened Version of Your Layered Image	80
If It's Not Square, You Can Still Crop It	80
Top-Secret Photoshop Splash Screen	81
Fall in Love with a Temporary Brush, or Not	81
Undo a Save? That's Impossible, Isn't It?	82
Make a Photoshop Client Presentation	82
Change Brush Softness on the Fly	83
Lights, Camera, Action: Slide Shows Using Photoshop	83
How to Correct One Problem Color	84
Building a Better Background Eraser Tool	85
Getting Side-by-Side Previews	86
Custom Brushes: Start with a Clean Slate	86
Timing Is Everything!	87
Instant Thumbnail Size Control	87
Bring Up Your Last Preference	88

CHAPTER 4   91
Burn Rubber
Smokin' Type Tips

Getting Type in a Perfect Circle	92
I Need My Dumb Quotes Again	92
Resetting Your Type	93
One-Click Access to the Copyright Symbol, and More	93
Highlighting Your Text Super Fast!	94
Rendering Text in Just One Click	94
Made to Fit	95
Text-Path-Making Maniac	95
Picture This: Putting a Photo inside Type	96
Fonts, Fonts, and More Fonts	97
Make Your Text Jump into Action	97
Double Your Pleasure	98
Seeing Your Type Change Color	98
Move Your Type, without Switching Tools	99

Editing Text without Highlighting It   99
Rasterize Times 2, 4, 6...   100
Honey, I Need Some Space: Visually Adjust Kerning   100
Tell Photoshop When You're Done with Type   101
Bring Those Type Layers Together   101
The Long and the Short of Type   102
Made to Fit: Part Two   102
Making the Spell Checker Obey Your Commands   103
Editing Type on a Path   103
Exact Sizing for Your Text Columns   104
Removing Those Typographically Incorrect Spaces   104
Tweak All Your Type in One Fell Swoop!   105
Don't Have Italic or Bold? Don't Sweat It   105

CHAPTER 5   107
Fast & Furious
Killer Web Tips

Lose Those Annoying Numbers in the Upper
   Left-Hand Corner   108
Need to Shrink the File Size? Use Transparency   108
Crop It Even Closer   109
Let Photoshop Make the File Size Call   109
Zoom Out for Sharper Web Images   110
ImageReady Feature Comes to Photoshop   110
Two Easy Ways to Create Transparency   111
ImageReady Window Speed Tip   111
If It's Web Safe, Don't Use It   112
Change One Preference, Save a Bundle   112
Get the Real 100% View   113
Style Warning for Web Designers   113
Spend More Time Animating, Less Time Clicking   114
Getting to the Hexadecimal Code   114
Get Super-Clean Type for the Web   115
Got a Folder Full of Images for the Web? Batch 'Em!   115
Exercising Your Influence on GIFs   116
Read the Web Color Onscreen   116
ImageReady's Supercharged Eyedropper   117
ImageReady's Auto Tile Maker   117
Make Sure You See It the Same Way They See It   118
Don't Load That Bogus Slice!   118
Use Layer-Based Slices   119
Blur That JPEG and Shrink It Down   119

CHAPTER 6   121
Fast Company
Photoshop Design Tips

Effective Ghosting or Backscreening   122

TABLE OF CONTENTS

Two-Color May Be Better Than Four   122
Overlap Graphic Elements to Add Visual Interest   123
Focusing Attention by Adding Depth   123
Focusing Attention Using Color   124
Don't Make It Black—Make It Mega Black!   124
Shadow Opacity and Softness   125
Create Your Own Custom Typeface   126
Use Correct CMYK Builds to Match Pantone Colors   126
Add Color to Your Shadows   127
Picking Colors? Use the Built-In Color Wheel   128
Color Combinations Affect Size and Proportion   129
Use Tight Cropping to Spice Up Images   129
Determining the Length of a Cast Shadow   130
Add a Point of Reference to Convey Size   131

CHAPTER 7   133
Speedy Gonzalez
Layer Tips

Almost a Built-In Flattening Shortcut   134
Jump to Any Layer Just by Clicking in Your Image   134
Turning Your Layers into Separate Documents   135
Opening Layered Files without All the Layers   135
Missing Your Background Layer? Here's the Fix   136
Avoiding the Layer Menu   136
Lock All Those Layers in Just One Click   137
Toggle Through the Blend Modes   137
Hide Your Other Layers in the Blink of an Eye   138
Why Dragging and Dropping Styles Rocks!   138
Applying Layer Styles to Your Background Layer   139
Turn Your Layer Comps into Their Own Docs   139
More Control over Blends: Advanced Blending   140
Instant Opacity Change   140
Copy a Layer in the Same Location in
    Another Document   141
Moving Multiple Layers from Document
    to Document   141
Centering Dragged Layers the Easy Way   142
Easier Drop Shadow Angle Adjustments   142
Layer Navigation Shortcut   143
Super-Fast Layer Copies   143
Instant Layer Alignment   144
Separation Anxiety: Put a Layer Style on
    a Separate Layer   144
Layer Effects Removal Speed Tip   145
Shapes without the Shape Layer   145
Color-Coding Made Easy   146
Can't Paint on a Layer? Here's Why   146
Speed Up Photoshop by Merging Layers   147

Layer Set Super-Speed Tip   147
Save Room in Your Layers Palette   148
Can't We All Just Have the Same Style?   149
Layer Palette Navigation Speed Tips   149
Quick-Copy Your Layer Mask   150
Select Everything on Your Layer in One Click   150
View Your Layer Mask as a Rubylith   151
Selecting Just One Object on a Layer   151
Keep Layer Styles from Affecting New Work   152
Un-Filling for Fun and Profit   153
Opacity Slider Speed Tips   153
Secret Opacity See-Through Part of a Layer Tip   154
Skipping the Layer Comp Dialog   155

CHAPTER 8   157
Speed Freak
Troubleshooting Tips

The Reappearing/Disappearing Brush Tip   158
Get Print Resolution from Your Digital Camera Images   158
How to Use RGB Filters on Grayscale Images   159
Stop the Crop Snapping   159
Let's Do the Text Warp Again   160
Unlocking the Background Layer   160
Trimming Your Plug-Ins for Faster Startup   161
Making Your Color Printouts Match Your Monitor   161
Do You Have Enough RAM? Ask Photoshop   162
Getting Better EPS Previews   162
The Killer Troubleshooting Tip: Deleting the Preferences   163
Get Back Your Background Layer   164
Expanding Rectangular Selections   164
Fixing the "Rounded Corners" Selection Problem   165
Making Global Light Work for You   165
Find the Hidden Magnetic Pen Tool Options   166
Printing Shadows over Solid Colors in Page Layout Apps   167
Let Photoshop Rebuild Your Prefs   168
Stop the "Click-and-Jump-to-That-Layer" Blues   168
Faster Application Switching   169
Will More RAM Make Photoshop Run Faster?   169
Don't Use Crop to Fix Barrel Distortion   170
Getting Smaller Photoshop Files   170
How to Use Actions from the Web   171

CHAPTER 9   173
Speed 2
Image-Correction and Prepress Tips

Getting More Accurate Color Using Replace Color   174
Correcting Highlights? Watch Out for Open Shadows!   174

TABLE OF CONTENTS

How to Heal on a Blank Layer   175
Better Healing with a Custom Brush   175
Creating a Custom Shadow/Highlight Default   176
Getting Back Shadow/Highlight's Factory Defaults   176
Healing with Pressure   177
Control the Opacity of Your Healing Process   177
Say Good-Bye to Gradient Banding   178
Sharpening Your Images Like a Pro   178
Five Tips for Getting Rid of Moiré Patterns   179
Scan Line Art at the Resolution You Need   180
Using the High Pass Filter for Sharpening   180
Spot Color Gradient Film Saver   181
Correct in CMYK or RGB?   181
Straightening Scans in 10 Seconds (or Less)   182
Stay Away from the Sponge Tool   182
Removing Noise in Digital Camera Images   183
Scanners Aren't Just for Flat Objects   183
Removing Red Eye with the Color Replace Brush   184
Are Your Colors Press Ready?   184
Never Swap Colors Again When Cleaning Line Art   185
Let Photoshop Do Your Resolution Math   185
Going to Press? Make Sure Your Monitor Is in
   the "Right Space"   186
Want Better Gradients on Press? Here's the Tip   186
Getting Before and After Previews   187
Cloning from Image to Image   187
Get More Realistic Drop Shadows on Press   188
Making Sure Your Whites Are Really White   188
Try Not to Correct More Than Once   189
Have Photoshop Help Find Your Highlights/Shadows   189
Talkin' 'Bout My Resolution   190
Are You Really Seeing Your Sharpening?   190
Adjusting Curve Points with Precision   191
Apply Unsharp Mask to CMYK Images   191
RGB Flesh Tones: Getting The "Red" Out   192
Once You're in CMYK Mode, Stay There   192
The Simple Tip to Better Color Separations   193
How to Sharpen Flesh Tones in CMYK   193
How to Read Four Areas at Once   194
More Curve Point Quick Tips   194

CHAPTER 10   197
Speed Kills
Advanced Tips

Using the File Browser to Open 16-Bit Images   198
Keeping Track of Your Every Move   198
Embed Your Message into Your Photos   199
Managing the Metadata Overload   199

Photoshop's Own Slide Show   200
The Histogram Palette's Visual Cues   200
Seeing Your Full-Color Image While Editing a Channel   201
How to Combine Two Paths into One   201
Power Up Your Layer Styles   202
Swapping Files? Make Sure Your Color Stays Intact   202
Freeform/Pen Tool Quick Switch   203
Visual Control over Your Selections Using Quick Mask   203
Better Color-to-Grayscale Using Lab   204
Have Photoshop Select the Shadows and Highlights   204
Troubleshooting Actions? Slow Down!   205
Accessing Grayed-Out Filters In CMYK   205
More Control over Filters   206
Assigning Metadata to Multiple Files   206
Applying Multiple Filters? Not on My Layer!   207
New Snapshot, the Mistake Insurance Policy   207
Saving Your Actions as Printable Text Files   208
3D Print Effects (and Where to Get Those Goofy Glasses)   208
Creating Reusable Diagonal Guides   209
Locking Your Tablet Brush Settings   209
The Secrets of Searching in the Browser   210
Drag-and-Drop Curves for Quick Correction   210
Actions Power Tip: Add an Action to Your Action   211
Prepress Cleanups—in a Snap   211
Blend Mode Power Tip   212
Making Changes to Raw Photos without Opening Them   212
No More Creating Type in Channels   213
Let Photoshop Tell You the Highlight and Shadow   213
Using the Lasso—Don't Stop to Navigate   214
Load Any Saved Selection without the
   Channels Palette   214
Plot Multiple Curve Points in Just One Click   215
Tough Selection Tip   215
Making the Color Picker Show CMYK   216
Moving Multiple Curve Points at Once   216
Add to Your Selections through the Channels Palette   217
Embedding Paths into Actions   217
Measure Twice, Look Once   218
Stroking Half a Path—Half a Path????   219
Speeding Up Batch Actions   219
Locking a PDF Presentation   220
Saving Time When Correcting Camera Raw Photos   220
Putting Your Lens Flare on the Spot   221

Index   222

INTRODUCTION

Why we wrote this book

The inspiration for this book came when Felix saw what the car payment would be on a new Porsche Boxster. He came to me and said, "Dude, I gotta write a book." Okay, you know we're kidding, but admit it—don't you secretly wish that for once, when someone was doing something strictly for the money, they'd just come out and say so. Just once, wouldn't you like to hear someone admit it? Well, I hate to disappoint you, but I can tell you unequivocally that Felix and I absolutely did not write this book for the money. We wrote it to get free drugs. All authors get free drugs—it's in every book contract. Always has been.

Actually, the reason we wanted to write this book is because of something that is already in almost every Photoshop book ever written: the tips. You know—those cool little tips littered throughout the sidebars of all great Photoshop books. We found that those little tips were often our favorite parts of the book. In fact, Felix and I agreed that frequently we'd read all those little sidebar tips first—before we'd ever sit down to actually read a chapter. It's those neat little tips that the great authors include that make using Photoshop so much fun (and make their books so great). The only problem is, there's just not enough of 'em.

So we thought, "Wouldn't it be cool if there was a Photoshop book where the whole book, cover-to-cover, was nothing but those little tips on the side!" Then Felix jumped up and yelled, "Let's write that book!" I jumped up and yelled, "Yes, yes! We have to write that book. It's our destiny!" Then Felix yelled, "Then I can get my Porsche!" I mean, he yelled, "This book will help humanity and be written for the common good" (or something like that. I can't remember. Probably because of all the drugs).

Is this book for you?

Is this book for you? Are you kidding? This book is so for you that it secretly freaks you out. Look, we don't know you personally, but we know Photoshop people. You're just like us—you love those little sidebar tips just as much as we do. If you didn't, authors would've stopped adding them to their books years ago, because, frankly, they're a pain in the butt to compile. But we know what you're thinking. Sure, you love those little tips—those inside secrets that make you look smart at parties and gain respect from your peers, homies, peeps, and other esteemed colleagues, but you want something more. You want the one thing that those cool little sidebar tips never seem to have. That's right, graphics. As cool as those sidebar tips are, they're always just a tiny little box with a couple of lines of text (like the sidebar we added above left). So we thought we'd expand the explanations just enough to make them more accessible, and add an accompanying graphic to enhance each tip's innate juiciness. They must remain "juicy." They must be "juicy tips."

Now you're probably wondering, "Guys, Photoshop is one amazing program with an unrivaled power and incredible depth. Couldn't you have come up with at least 1,000 Photoshop tips?" Absolutely. We could have included loads of tips, such as "F7 brings up the Layers palette," and "Press G-Shift-G to get the Paint Bucket tool," but the problem is, those aren't "Killer Tips." Every Photoshop book has those tips. Heck, books about gardening probably even have those Photoshop tips. For a tip to get in this book, it had to be a "Killer Tip." Each tip had to be one that would make the reader smile, nod, and then pick up the phone to call another Photoshop user just to "tune them up" with their newfound power. Remember, these are killer tips, so be careful. Someone could get hurt.

TIP

This is a sidebar tip. Every great Photoshop book has a few of them. But this book is nothing but them. A whole book of cool sidebar tips, without the sidebars.

Okay, how do I get started?

In my previous Photoshop books *Photoshop CS Down & Dirty Tricks* and *The Photoshop CS Book for Digital Photographers*, I used a technique that really worked well. I gratuitously mentioned my other books in the introduction, just in case I didn't get to plug them later. No, wait… that's not it. What I did tell the reader was that my books aren't set up like a novel. They're purposely not designed to make you start at Chapter One and read your way through to the back (where hopefully, I'll again have an opportunity to plug, I mean casually mention, my other books). Instead, this book is designed so you can jump in anywhere, in any chapter, and immediately try the tips that interest you the most, regardless of your level of experience in Photoshop. You don't need to load any special images from a CD-ROM or go to a Web site to download special photos—these are just cool tips. No flaming type, no multilevel glows—just timesaving shortcuts and efficiency tips that will make you faster and better at Photoshop than you'd ever thought you'd be.

Also, like my previous books, we spell out everything. So if you've been using Photoshop for years, don't let it frustrate you because instead of just writing, "Create a new layer," we usually write, "Create a new layer by clicking on the New Layer icon at the bottom of the Layers palette." We do that because we want everyone, at any skill level, to be able to open the book to any page and start applying these cool tips to their work immediately.

This book is built on the premise that "Speed Kills." Because after all, if you get faster at Photoshop, you'll have more time to be creative, and the more time you spend being creative, the more fun you'll have.

Is this book for Macintosh, Windows, or both?

This book is not only for Mac and Windows users, it's for people who don't even have a computer. In fact, it's ideal for anyone with $29.99 (kidding). Because Photoshop is identical on both the Macintosh and Windows operating systems, the book is for both Mac and Windows users. However, the keyboards on a Mac and PC are slightly different, so every time we give a keyboard shortcut, we give both the Mac and Windows shortcuts. (Well, there is one other difference— in Mac OS X you'll find Photoshop's Preferences under the new Photoshop menu instead of the Edit menu like it used to be in the Mac OS and still is in Windows.)

How to use this book

This book is designed to be read while moving at a high rate of speed. If you're barreling down the highway going 80 mph, weaving in and out of traffic, that's the ideal time to turn to Chapter Six to read the tip on "How to assist EMS workers with using the Jaws of Life." Okay, admittedly, that's probably not a good idea, so instead, just make sure you open this book in front of your computer so you can dive right into the tips. Remember, the one who dies with the most cool tips wins.

What not to do

You're almost ready to get to the tips, but first a word of caution: "Caution." There. Now you're ready. Actually, we did want to point out that the only two actual sidebar tips in the entire book are on these two pages. So, don't go rippin' through the book looking for all those little sidebar tips, because we intentionally left the sidebars blank. Why? So we could write another book called *The Missing Killer Tips Sidebars*, just in case Felix ever sees what the payment is for a house on the beach.

TIP

You're doing it again! Stop looking at these sidebars. See, they're intoxicating—you're drawn to them even after you know it's not really a tip. Okay, here's a real tip: If you like sidebar tips, buy this book.

Life in the Fast Lane

PRODUCTION TIPS

Imagine a pig. Wait, not the sloppy grunting kind. Imagine that cute pig from the movie Babe. *Clean, well-kempt, with a broad vocabulary and a slightly*

Life in the Fast Lane
production tips

British accent. Ahh, that's better. Now, imagine that he somehow stumbled into a giant vat of grease, jumped out, and began to run at full speed. If you decided to try and catch him with your bare hands (and it's a reasonable assumption that you would), how easy would that be?

Now, think of this chapter as "the making of the pig." But now you're the pig, and your competition is trying to catch you. But after learning the tips in this chapter, you're "faster than a greased pig" in Photoshop. Okay, I admit this whole pig thing isn't the greatest metaphor. Let's try this. You're an eagle, a soaring proud bird. And you've somehow fallen into a giant vat of grease. Suddenly, a shot rings out…. I'm not sure I like where this is going.

Let's try this: Every day you spend time in Photoshop. Some of it is fun, creative time. Some of it is boring production time, such as making selections, loading brush sets, applying Curves, cropping, transforming—you know, boring stuff. But if you could greatly speed up the boring stuff, that would leave more time for the fun, creative stuff, right? When you strip away all the greased-pig metaphors, that's what this chapter is really about. Run, Babe, run!

MAKING THE PREVIEW PALETTE BIGGER

Want a taller preview in the File Browser for photos taken in a portrait orientation (tall rather than wide)? Just double-click on the Folders tab, and it will "roll up," and the Preview palette will expand upward into the Folders space, giving you a preview that's twice as tall.

   SAVING FILE BROWSER SETUPS

In Photoshop CS, your custom File Browser setups can be saved as Workspaces, which opens a new way of working within the File Browser. For example, if you shoot a lot of portraits, you can double-click on the Folders

tab (to roll it up out of the way, giving you a taller Preview palette), then drag the divider bar between the palettes area and the thumbnail area to the right to make your preview even bigger. Since your preview is so large, you can shrink the size of your thumbnails (go to the View menu in the File Browser and choose Medium Thumbnail). Once you've done all this, save this setup as a Workspace by going to the Window menu, under Workspace, and choosing Save Workspace (name it "File Browser Portrait"). Then, next time you're looking through some proofs, you can have huge previews in just one click. You can do the same thing for wide photos—just drag the divider bar much farther to the right, until the preview of photos with a landscape orientation takes up most of the File Browser Screen. Now switching between huge portrait and landscape previews only takes one click.

SETTING DEFAULTS IN THE FILTER GALLERY

Believe it or not, there's a hidden "Default" button within the Filter Gallery that lets you set up and save your own custom default settings so each time you open the Filter Gallery, it has your favorite settings already in place. Here's how to set your defaults: Open the Filter Gallery (found under the Filter menu), set it up just the way you want, then hold the Command key (PC: Control key) and you'll notice that the Cancel button changes into the Default button. Click on that and your current settings now become the default settings.

 REARRANGING YOUR BRUSHES

One of the things in Photoshop that just didn't make sense to us was that you couldn't easily rearrange the order of your brushes in the Brushes palette. Oh sure, you could create a whole new custom set with the brushes you wanted, in the order you wanted them, but it would take a while, and frankly, was such a pain that we only know a handful of people who actually went through the trouble. Well, our wish for easily rearranging brushes is finally here, but the process is a bit hidden beneath the surface. To move a brush from one spot in the palette to

another, go under the Edit menu, and choose Preset Manager. In the Preset Manager dialog, under Preset Type, choose Brushes. Then, click-and-drag the brush of your choice to the location of your choice. At last, we are free to move brushes among the herd.

CREATING YOUR OWN CUSTOM NEW DOCUMENT PRESETS

If you're creating new documents and find yourself using the same new document sizes fairly often (for example, let's say that you wind up creating a new document that's 7″ wide by 5″ tall, at a resolution of 225, in CMYK mode), you can make that a preset in the New dialog of Photoshop CS (technically, you could do this in Photoshop 7 by hacking a text document, but it was a bit of a pain, and most people didn't do it). To create your own presets, just go under the File menu, chose New, then in the New dialog, enter your favorite settings, then press the Save Preset button. A dialog will appear where you can name your preset, and when you click OK, that preset will be saved to the New dialog Preset menu near the top of the list.

   FIND THE CENTER OF ANY DOCUMENT

Need to find the exact center of your image? All you need is a layer filled with your Foreground color, and Photoshop will do the rest (okay, you have to do a little, but Photoshop will certainly help). First, create a new layer and fill it with your Foreground color. Make your rulers visible and drag a guide down from the top ruler. When you get close to the center of the image, the guide will automatically snap to the exact horizontal center. Do the same with the side ruler, and it automatically snaps to the vertical center of your image. (Note: If there's not any snapping going on, make sure that Snap is turned on under the View menu.)

NO MORE JAGGY LASSO TOOL SELECTIONS

Have you ever tried to create a smooth selection using the Lasso tool? It's just about impossible, right? (If it sounds like it isn't, give it a try—open a new document, take the Lasso tool, and draw any random selection, and then look at the selection. It's jaggy—not crazy jaggy, but it's certainly not smooth.) If you were trying to create a selection for an interface design, or a realistic element of some sort, it would just be too jaggy to use. Here's a tip:

(1) Draw around the area you want to use as your selection with the Lasso tool.

(2) Press the letter "q" to enter Quick Mask mode (your selection will now be surrounded by solid pink).

(3) Go under the Filter menu, under Noise, and choose Median. As you raise the Radius of the Median filter, you'll see your edges smooth out.

(4) When it looks nice and smooth, click OK, then press the letter "q" again to return to Standard mode, and you'll have nothing but a nice smooth selection.

Look at the selection in the first image above. See how those jaggies have been replaced by the smooth edges—courtesy of the Median filter?

THE MENU TO FULL SCREEN MODE

There have always been two ways to get to Full Screen Mode—you either knew the hidden keyboard shortcut (f, f, then tab) or you clicked on the third icon near the bottom of the Toolbox (but that still didn't hide the palettes; you had to know to press the Tab key to do that). Well, in Photoshop CS it's gotten easier because the different screen modes are now found by going under the View menu, under Screen Mode. However, even though choosing Full Screen Mode does hide the menu bar, it doesn't hide the palettes. You still have to press the Tab key for that.

EXPERIMENTING WITH ZOOM

If you're not sure what amount of zoom (magnification) you want for your current image, here's a tip that will save you some time. Type the first zoom percentage in the Zoom field (in the bottom left-hand corner of your document window), but once you've entered it, don't just press Enter to see the zoom, press Shift-Enter. That way, the Zoom field stays highlighted so if you don't like the amount of zoom, you can just type in a new percentage, without manually re-targeting that field. A big time saver!

OPEN UP SOME SCREEN REAL ESTATE

A lot of times when you're working on a project, your screen can get really cluttered with palettes (Photoshop is an especially palette-heavy application). If you want all the palettes out of the way for your convenience while you're working, just press Shift-Tab to hide them, or Shift-Tab to bring them back. The menu bar, the Options Bar, and the Toolbox will all still be visible.

LET PHOTOSHOP DO THE WORK IN CURVES

Let's say you're using the Curves dialog for correcting images and you have an image where you're trying to adjust the color of some green plants. How do you know where that particular green "lives" on the curve so you can dial in and adjust it? Photoshop can tell you—in fact, you can have Photoshop automatically plot that color on the curve for you. With the Curves dialog open, just Command-click (PC: Control-click) on that color within your image. Photoshop will then add a point to the curve that represents the spot you sampled, and now you're ready to tweak it.

  WANT A FINER GRID? YOU GOT IT!

While we're talking Curves, by default the Curves dialog displays a 25% grid (shown above left). If you'd like a finer grid, you can Option-click (PC: Alt-click) once within the grid, and it will then display a 10% grid (shown above right).

YOU DON'T NEED THE BRUSHES PALETTE TO CHANGE BRUSH SIZE

In Photoshop CS you can increase/decrease the size of your brush by 10 pixels by pressing the Left or Right Bracket keys. Once your brush goes over 100 pixels in size, it then moves in 25-pixel increments, and if you go over 200 pixels it moves in 50-pixel increments until you reach 300, at which point it moves in 100-pixel increments.

   ## ROTATE TO ANY ANGLE THE FAST WAY

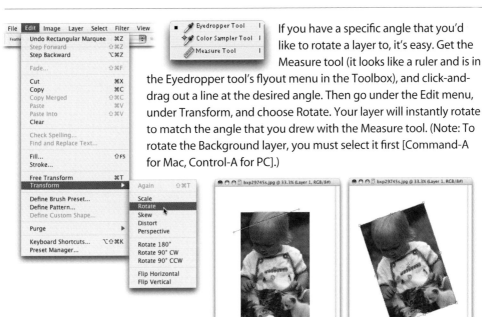

If you have a specific angle that you'd like to rotate a layer to, it's easy. Get the Measure tool (it looks like a ruler and is in the Eyedropper tool's flyout menu in the Toolbox), and click-and-drag out a line at the desired angle. Then go under the Edit menu, under Transform, and choose Rotate. Your layer will instantly rotate to match the angle that you drew with the Measure tool. (Note: To rotate the Background layer, you must select it first [Command-A for Mac, Control-A for PC].)

REMOVING POINTS FROM THE POLYGONAL LASSO

When you're using the Polygonal Lasso tool, every time you click to change directions, it automatically lays down a point where you pivoted. If you added a point and didn't mean to, you can delete it by pressing the Delete (PC: Backspace) key. Every time you press Delete (PC: Backspace), it deletes another previous point (in the order they were created). In fact, if you really mess up, you can keep pressing Delete until you're right back where you started.

   ## GETTING TO THE RIGHT PALETTE JUST GOT EASIER

This sounds like such a little thing that you'll wonder why Adobe didn't do it years ago, but now the list of palettes under the Window menu is in alphabetical order. I know what you're thinking. They weren't in alphabetical order all along? Nope. But they are now—no more digging around to find the right palette. Sounds simple, and it is.

OPENING AN IMAGE AND CLOSING THE FILE BROWSER

One thing that really adds to your desktop clutter is the fact that when you open a photo from the File Browser, the File Browser remains open behind your photo. In most cases, you can still see the top, right-hand side, bottom, or all three (depending on the size of your photo) peeking out from behind your photo. But it doesn't have to be that way. To open a photo, and have Photoshop automatically close the File Browser, don't just double-click on the thumbnail to open it; instead, Option-double-click (PC: Alt-double-click) on the thumbnail.

OPENING MULTIPLE IMAGES AND CLOSING THE BROWSER

Want to open multiple photos at once and have Photoshop close the File Browser for you? Just Command-click (PC: Control-click) on all the photos you want to open, then press Option-Return (PC: Alt-Enter). All the selected photos will open, and the File Browser will close.

GET RID OF UNWANTED BRUSHES

You probably already know that you can add a brush to the Brushes palette, but did you know that it's even easier to delete them? Just hold the Option key (PC: Alt key) and you'll notice that your cursor changes into a pair of scissors (as shown at left on the 13-pixel, soft-edged brush). Click once on the brush you want to delete and that baby's gone—no warning dialog, no chance to change your mind—it's gone.

NAVIGATING THE BRUSH PICKER LIKE A PRO

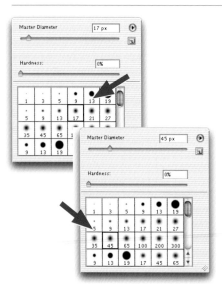

Now that you've learned how to bring up the Brush Picker right where you want it, it wouldn't hurt to learn this quick navigation tip to keep you from spending more time there than is necessary. Once you've selected a brush in the Picker, just use the Arrow keys on your keyboard to navigate up, down, left, or right to other brushes. Once you choose a brush and you are no longer in the Brush Picker, you can use the Period and Comma keys to move forward and backward through the different brushes. Shift-Comma and Shift-Period will jump you to the first and last brushes in the Brushes palette, respectively.

GET MORE CONTROL OVER YOUR PAINT STROKES

Photoshop lets you affect a brush stroke even after you've painted it by using Photoshop's Fade command (found under the Edit menu). Fade works like "undo on a slider," and dragging the Opacity slider all the way to the left will completely undo your freshly painted brush stroke, but if you stop anywhere before the far left side, it will instead give you a percentage of undo, lightening your stroke. You can also use the pop-up Mode menu to alter how your stroke blends with the object below it.

  SPEED TIP TO ROTATE THROUGH OPEN IMAGES

This tip has been in the Windows version of Photoshop for quite some time, but since Photoshop 6.0, Macintosh users can do it too—press Control-Tab to move from one open image to the next, rotating through to any of your open documents.

INSTANTLY FIND THE CENTER OF ANY OBJECT

This is a great tip for quickly finding the exact center of any object on its own layer. You start by pressing Command-T (PC: Control-T) to bring up the Free Transform bounding box. The bounding box has a handle in the center of both sides and center handles at both the top and bottom. Now all you have to do is make Photoshop's rulers visible (Command-R on Mac, Control-R on PC), and then drag out a horizontal and a vertical ruler guide to these handles to mark the center.

   ## MAKING YOUR GUIDE FLIP

Just like most page layout applications, Photoshop has non-printing guides you can pull out anytime you need to align objects (or type as shown at left), but there's also a trick for flipping the guides. To access the guides, make your rulers visible by pressing Command-R (PC: Control-R), then click-and-hold within one of the rulers and drag out a guide. If you pull out a horizontal guide from the top ruler, but really wanted a vertical guide, just press the Option key (PC: Alt key) and your guide will flip from horizontal to vertical (pretty slick). You can pull out as many guides as you need (there's probably a limit to how many you can use, but we've never reached it). When you're done using a guide, just use the Move tool to drag it back to the ruler where it came from. To remove all of your guides at once, choose Clear Guides from the View menu.

CREATING TEMPORARY BRUSHES

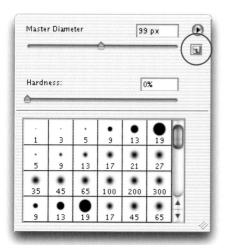

It's easy to create a temporary brush based on your preset brushes in Photoshop CS. Just click on the Brush Sample in the Options Bar to bring up the Brushes Picker. With the Master Diameter slider you can change your brush size from 1 to 2500 pixels. If you like the size of your new brush and you want to save it, just click the New Brush icon at the top right of the dialog. The Brush Name dialog will appear so you can name your new brush. When you click OK, the new brush will immediately be added to your Brushes palette.

   REUSING YOUR LAST CURVE SETTING

Once you've applied a curve setting to an image, it's very possible that you'd like to use that exact same setting again, or maybe you'd just like to tweak that setting a bit. Well, you can. To bring up the Curves dialog with the last curve you used still in place, press Option-Command-M (PC: Alt-Control-M).

BRINGING BACK THOSE CROPPED-AWAY AREAS

When you're using the Crop tool to crop images, you'll find that you actually have some options on how the area you're cropping away is handled after the crop. For example, in the Options Bar (as long as you're not on the Background layer) you'll see an option that lets you either Delete the cropped areas or simply Hide them from view (in other words, the areas are still there, they just expand out into the Canvas area). If you choose the Hide option, it crops the image window down to the size of the crop, but since the cropped-away areas are still really there, you can use the Move tool to drag these cropped areas back into view.

   FIX THOSE STRAY PIXELS FAST!

Sometimes when making a selection with the Magic Wand tool or Color Range (under the Select menu), Photoshop will leave little stray pixels unselected. You can tell where they are because they appear to twinkle on and off, kind of teasing…nay, taunting you, because your selection is not complete. Luckily, there's a quick way to rein in those renegade stray pixels. Go under the Select menu, under Modify, and choose Smooth. Enter a Sample Radius of 1 pixel and click OK. That will usually do the trick—those stray pixels are now selected.

GETTING MORE CONTROL OVER THE MAGIC WAND

By default, the Eyedropper tool's Sample Size option (in the Options Bar) is set to Point Sample, which comes into play if you're using it to read values for color correction. But for now, it's important to know that the Sample Size option chosen for the Eyedropper tool actually affects how the Magic Wand tool makes its selection (the two have an undocumented relationship). If you increase the Eyedropper's Sample Size to 3 by 3 or 5 by 5 Average, the Magic Wand will select an average of a much larger range of pixels in the sample area. This is important to know, because if you don't have Point Sample chosen and you set the Magic Wand Tolerance to 0, it won't just select the individual pixel you click on—it will select all of the pixels that match any of the pixels in a 3 by 3 or 5 by 5 area. The next time your Magic Wand isn't behaving the way it used to, check and see if you have changed the Eyedropper tool's Sample Size.

   ## MAKING THE COLOR PALETTE WORK TWICE AS HARD

If you use the Color palette to select colors, you're probably already using the color ramp at the bottom of the palette for making quick color selections, but here are two tips that make using the ramp faster and easier. First, the color ramp doesn't have to use the same color mode as the color sliders above it; for example, you can have RGB for your sliders and grayscale as your ramp. This is great because it gives you two different models to choose from without digging through menus. You can choose the color modes for both the sliders and the ramp from the Color palette's pop-down menu. The second tip is that if you want to change color ramps quickly, Shift-click on the ramp. Every time you click, it will rotate through to the next color mode.

PHOTOSHOP REMEMBERS THE LAST SIZE YOU INPUT

Although there's no way to set a default size for your New document dialog (outside of creating an action to do it for you), there's a pretty cool little-known tip that lets you open a new document using the last settings you manually input. Just press Option-Command-N (PC: Alt-Control-N) and the New document dialog will appear using the last settings you input (rather than using the clipboard data to determine the new document size).

   SEEING YOUR CURVES UP CLOSE

For some weird reason, the trendy thing to do now is to use a monitor display setting that makes your icons so small, it's really just about a blind guess as to which program or file you're clicking (or double-clicking) on. This becomes more of a problem when you're doing a Curves adjustment, because the dialog that once looked so huge at 640x480 pixels now looks tiny at 1280x960. But fear not: Adobe added a tiny, innocent-looking button at the bottom right-hand corner of the Curves dialog, and when you click on it, it gives you a significantly larger version of Curves so you can finally see what you're doing. By the way, if your menus are so small you can't read them, this will help—the keyboard shortcut for Curves is Command-M (PC: Control-M). Sorry, that last part was sass. Total sass. Mega-sass. I feel really bad about it.

USE YOUR LAST SETTINGS AND SAVE TIME

This is a tip that will save you time when you're making tonal adjustments using Levels, Curves, Color Balance, etc. (most anything that appears under the Adjustments menu under the Image menu). When you bring up one of the tonal adjustment dialogs, it always displays its default settings, but if you hold the Option key (PC: Alt key) when choosing it from the Adjustments menu, instead of coming up with the default settings, it will display the last settings you used in that particular dialog. You can also add the Option (PC: Alt) key to the keyboard shortcuts. For example, the shortcut to bring up the Levels dialog is Command-L (PC: Control-L), but if you add Option (PC: Alt) to those keys, the Levels dialog will open with your last-used settings.

HIT THOSE CHANNELS FAST

When you're in the Curves dialog, if you're charging by the hour, you can certainly travel up to the Channel pop-up menu and choose each individual channel you want to work on, but if you want to do it the fast way, just press Command-1 for Red, Command-2 for Green, and Command-3 for Blue (PC: Control-1, Control-2, etc.). If you need to return to the composite RGB channel, press Command-Tilde (PC: Control-Tilde). By the way, the Tilde key looks like ~, and it lives right above the Tab key on your keyboard. Don't feel bad. Nobody knows what the Tilde key is. We're not sure it's a real symbol at all. We think it was made up so there wouldn't be an empty space there on your keyboard. Hey, it's somewhat plausible.

HOW TO GET AN UNDO AFTER YOU'VE CLOSED THE DOCUMENT

As you probably already know, the History palette keeps track of the last 20 changes to your document that you can use for multiple undos when working on a project. The only bad part is that when you close your document, your undos (in History) are automatically deleted. However, there is a way to save an undo, as long as it's a tonal adjustment (such as Curves, Levels, Color Balance, etc.), by creating Adjustment layers. Just click on the half-white, half-black circle at the bottom of the Layers palette and choose your tonal adjustment from the pop-up menu to create an Adjustment layer. These Adjustment layers are saved as layers, along with your file. That way, the next time you open the file, you can go back and edit your Curves, Levels, etc. adjustment by double-clicking on the Adjustment layer. The last applied adjustment will appear, and you can edit it live. If you decide you don't want the original adjustment applied at all, you can drag the Adjustment layer into the Trash icon at the bottom of the Layers palette. You can also add a Gradient fill, a Pattern fill, and even a Solid Color fill as an Adjustment layer, giving you an undo at a later date, because again, they're saved as layers with the file.

   USING THE PEN? STAY AWAY FROM THE TOOLBOX

Want to save trips to the Toolbox when using the Pen tool? You're in luck. Better yet, you don't even have to hold down any modifier keys (such as Option/Alt, etc.), because Photoshop will do the work for you. Here's why: When you draw a path, move your cursor over a line segment, and your Pen cursor automatically changes to the Add Anchor Point tool so you can click anywhere along that path to add a point. Move your cursor over an existing point, and it changes into the Delete Anchor Point tool (click on the point, and it's deleted). This is called "Auto Add/Delete," and it's on by default (you can turn if off, should you want to, using the checkbox in the Options Bar).

PUT YOUR GRADIENT PICKER AT YOUR FINGERTIPS

Want to make the Gradient Picker appear under your cursor in your image window? You can do this, and have access to your gradient library by Control-clicking within your image area (PC: Right-click). It also works with the Custom Shape Picker. Here's an even slicker trick: You can use the Return or Enter key instead to bring up the Gradient or Custom Shape Pickers.

   DON'T CLICK IN THAT FIELD!

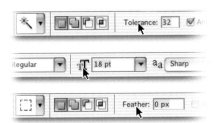

Those tiny little fields up in the Options Bar can really be a pain sometimes, especially if you're trying to highlight a field, delete the current value, and type in a new one. Instead of doing all that, just click on the field's name and Photoshop will automatically highlight the entire field for you. That way, you can just type in new values and it will automatically replace the old values. Great thing is, this doesn't just work in the Options Bar; it works in many of Photoshop's palettes, including the Character and Paragraph palettes.

OUT OF MEMORY? TRY THIS FIRST

Here's a tip for avoiding those nasty out-of-memory warning dialogs. One of the reasons Photoshop needs so much memory is that by default it keeps a snapshot of the last 20 things you did to your document, thus allowing you to undo your previous 20 steps. (You can see the running list of your last 20 steps in the History palette.) As you might expect, storing 20 steps takes a mighty chunk of memory, and if you're running a little low (or getting those evil out-of-memory warnings), one thing you might try is lowering the amount of steps Photoshop stores. In Mac OS X, go under the Photoshop menu, under Preferences, under General, and you'll find a field for History States. (In Windows you'll find Preferences under the Edit menu.) You can lower this number (try 8 States for starters), and you may avoid the dreaded memory warnings. Just remember, by lowering the States, you don't have 20 undos anymore.

   HOW TO "UNERASE"

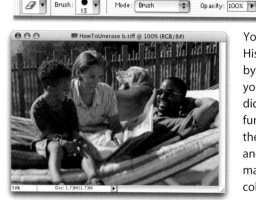

You probably already know that you can use the History Brush as an "undo" on a brush, and that by default, the History Brush paints back to how your image looked when you first opened it. But did you know that the Eraser tool has a similar function? That's right; the next time you've got the Eraser tool chosen, look up in the Options Bar and you'll see a checkbox for Erase to History. Normally, the Eraser tool erases to your Background color, but when you turn on this checkbox, it erases back to what the image looked like when you opened it.

LET PHOTOSHOP STRAIGHTEN YOUR CROOKED SCANS

That's right—straightening is totally automated in Photoshop CS. In fact, you can simply toss two or three photos casually onto your scanner bed, without taking the time to carefully align them, and scan them all with just one pass of your scanner. Then, open the single scan of the three photos in Photoshop, go under the File menu, under Automate, and choose Crop and Straighten Photos. Photoshop will then crop, straighten, and even put each photo into its own separate document. Nice.

   ## COPY ONE LAYER, OR COPY 'EM ALL

If you're working on a layered document and you make a selection and copy that selection, by default Photoshop copies only the information on your currently active layer (and that's a good thing). However, there may be times when you want to copy your selection as if the image was flattened (in other words, you want to copy everything on all visible layers). If that's the case, press Shift-Command-C (PC: Shift-Control-C), and you'll copy as if the image was flattened, not just on the active layer.

STUCK IN A FIELD? HERE'S HOW TO ESCAPE

This is one of those tips that keeps you from pulling your hair out. Sometimes when you're editing values in a field (for example, you're typing in Opacity numbers for a layer) and you've entered the number you want, Photoshop doesn't automatically take you out of that field (meaning your cursor is still flashing in the Opacity field). It gets worse if you've switched to any other layer (besides the Background layer) and you want to use a keyboard shortcut to switch tools. For example, you press the letter "t" to switch to the Type tool, but instead of getting the Type tool, you get an error "bong" because your cursor is still in the Opacity field and you can't type letters in a number field. Here's how to get around it. Just press the Return (Enter) key on your keyboard to lock in the change in your field and release your keyboard for other tasks.

   ## DON'T CANCEL; RESET AND SAVE TIME

Most of Photoshop's dialogs (but not all) will let you use this little tip, which can save you loads of time. When you're making changes in a dialog (let's use the Levels dialog as an example) and decide that you don't like the changes you've made, one option is to press the Cancel button to close the dialog, leaving your image unchanged. Then you can reopen the dialog and try again. This is an incredible waste of valuable time, so instead, Photoshop lets you "reset" the dialog—putting the settings back to what they were when you first opened it. Just hold the Option key (PC: Alt key) and look at the Cancel button—it changes into the Reset button. Click it, and it resets the dialog automatically, as if you hadn't made any changes at all. Big, big time saver.

TIME FOR SOME PANTONE CONVENIENCE

If you're using Pantone colors often in your work, you'll kill a lot of time if you pick your colors by clicking on the Color Swatches in the Toolbox to bring up the Color Picker, and then click on the Custom button to bring up the Custom Color Picker where you can type in the number of the Pantone color you want (if you're lucky enough to know that number off the top of your head. If not, then you'll have to scroll through the Pantone Color Picker). But there's a faster, easier way—load the Pantone colors into your Swatches palette. You do that by opening the Swatches palette (found under the Window menu), and in the palette's pop-down menu, choose Pantone Solid Coated. A dialog will appear asking whether you want to add (Append) these Pantone colors to your existing swatches or replace the current swatches with the Pantone set (I'd choose to replace, but hey, that's just me). Then, in the palette's pop-down menu, choose Small List to display both a swatch and the color's Pantone number.

   HOW TO HIDE THE PATH AROUND YOUR SHAPE

When you're using the Shape tool, by default it creates a Shape layer (and there are a number of reasons why you might want that) with a path around the shape. Most of the time, you don't need to see the path border around your shape (unless, of course, you want to edit that border), so to hide it from view, press Shift-Command-H (PC: Shift-Control-H).

ZOOMING IN THE FILTER GALLERY

Although you'll find a pop-up menu for choosing your preview zoom percentage in Photoshop CS's Filter Gallery, there's a much faster way to zoom in. Just use Command-+ (PC: Control-+) to zoom in, and Command-– (minus) (PC: Control-–) to zoom back out. Also, if you want a larger preview area, just grab the bottom right-hand corner of the preview window and drag outward, and the window will expand, giving you a much larger preview. Also try pressing Command-0 (PC: Control-0) and the Filter Gallery dialog will expand to take up your full screen.

   ## SEE EVERY TWEAK WITH BIGGER FILTER GALLERY PREVIEWS

Once you've chosen the Filter Gallery filters you want to apply, you'll probably want to spend some time tweaking their settings. If that's the case, you'd probably also like to have a bigger preview so you can really see the effects of each little tweak. You can do that by clicking on the up-facing triangle button, to the left of the OK button. This hides the center column (the list of filters) and expands the Preview column into its space, giving you a huge preview so you can see every tweak.

SHOWING ONE EFFECT IN THE FILTER GALLERY

The idea behind the Filter Gallery is the stacking up of one filter on top of the next, but if you want to see any one of the filters by itself, just Option-click (PC: Alt-click) on the Eye icon beside that filter in the filter stack, and all the other filters will be hidden from view. Option-click (PC: Alt-click) on the same Eye icon to bring them all back into view.

   ## USE THE MOVE TOOL ANYTIME

When you're using just about any of Photoshop's tools, you can temporarily switch to the Move tool at any time by simply holding the Command key (PC: Control key). It's temporary, and as soon as you release it, you're back to the tool you started with.

FILTER GALLERY ZOOM QUICK TIP

If you're in the Filter Gallery and want to zoom quickly to a particular level of magnification, just Control-click (PC: Right-click) anywhere within the Preview window and a pop-up list of zoom views will appear.

   TRASHING FILTER GALLERY FILTERS THE FAST WAY

Want to delete a filter fast? Don't waste time dragging it all the way to the Trash icon at the bottom of the Gallery. Just click on the filter—click on the Trash icon—it's gone!

SAVING YOUR FAVORITE FOLDERS IN THE FILE BROWSER

If, like most users, you find yourself going to the same fold-ers again and again (for example, if you keep all your photos in a Pictures folder, or in a common folder on your hard drive), you can now eliminate digging through the Folders palette to get to them. The next time you're in your photos folder, just go under the File Browser's File menu and choose Add Folder to Favorites. From now on, this folder will appear in the File Browser's Location pop-up menu, listed under Favorite Folders. Now your favorite folders are just one click away.

   ## NESTING YOUR FILE BROWSER PALETTES

Nesting palettes (putting commonly used palettes together in one palette, with just their tabs showing) is very popular in Photoshop, but you've never been able to do that within the File Browser. That is, until Photoshop CS. Now, you can do just that by dragging the tab of one palette up to another palette (just like you would outside the File Browser). For example, if you'd like all four File Browser palette tabs side by side up at the top of the File Browser's first column, just drag the lower three tabs up to the Folders palette, one by one.

BRUSHES RIGHT WHERE YOU WANT 'EM

Here's a tip that gives you a faster and more convenient way to switch to another preset brush without using the Brushes palette—and you might find that you like it even better. Just press the Control key, then click within your image (PC: Right-click) and the Brush Picker will appear directly under your cursor. Plus, you can even change the Master Diameter of the brush that you choose in the Picker. This is one you'll have to try to appreciate the sheer speed and convenience of putting your brushes at your fingertips anytime.

Born to Run

ESSENTIAL TIPS
YOU'VE GOT TO KNOW

Have you ever been to one of those trendy Photoshop parties? You know the ones I mean—where the guests sit around in the study, ensconced

Born to Run

essential tips you've got to know

in big leather chairs, smoking smuggled Cuban cigars, and casually chatting about "calculating this, and masking that…," and they keep referring to the time they were out on their yacht with Deke, Ben, and Jack. Don't you hate those parties? Me too. But nonetheless, I don't want to get caught at one of them and be the only goober there who didn't know that Shift-Delete is the undocumented shortcut for bringing up the Fill dialog. Imagine the shame. Then you'd have to pull that old, "Oh, I knew that. I thought you were referring to something in the Curves dialog that I heard at RIT," as they all slowly look away, rolling their eyes, glancing at each other with that "who's the spaz?" look on their faces. Do you want to be that person? Do you want to be that spaz? No? Then read this chapter, dammit. Memorize every word, every line, every keyboard shortcut. Then fire up a fat boy and head for the study. It's time to find a spaz to tease until he's in the fetal position.

THE HIDDEN MEASUREMENT POP-DOWN MENU

You probably already know the trick about entering values in measurement fields in the Options Bar. You can change your unit of measure by typing in the appropriate abbreviation after the value (for example, if you want 100 pixels, you'd type in "100 px"). But there's an even easier way (and you don't have to memorize a bunch of abbreviations). Just type in your number, Control-click (PC: Right-click) in the field, and a pop-up list of measurement units will appear. Just choose the one you want and it'll take care of the rest.

   BATCH RENAMING MADE MORE USABLE

Adobe added just one tiny field to the Batch Rename dialog in Photoshop CS. It hasn't gotten a lot of press, and it's not a real splashy feature, but this tiny field is worth its weight in gold if you do much batch renaming. The limitation has always been that if you added a serial number to one batch of photos (let's say you named them 1 to 54), if you added another batch of photos of the same subject, you couldn't start with the number 55. But now you can. That little field is found in the bottom left-hand corner of the dialog, and it's called "Starting Serial #." Once again—it's the little things, isn't it?

CHANGING METADATA FONT SIZES

If you're older than 17, chances are you'll find the font size Adobe uses for the Metadata palette way, way too small. Luckily, Adobe doesn't have many 17-year-olds on the payroll, so they included a way to increase the font size for the metadata. Just click on the little round button on the top-right side of the Metadata palette (it has a black, right-facing triangle in it)

and choose Increase Font Size from the pop-up menu. The cool thing is—you can choose this command more than once, making your font size bigger and bigger each time you choose it.

   GETTING A FRESH HISTOGRAM IN ONE CLICK

When you have the Histogram palette open to monitor your tonal adjustments to an image, you may see a tiny warning symbol in the right corner of your histogram. That's its way of letting you know that you're looking at a Histogram reading from the Histogram's memory cache—not a fresh reading. If you want to refresh the Histogram and get a new reading (and you should), you can click directly on the tiny warning symbol and it will refresh immediately for you.

USING THE LASSO TOOL? KEEP IT STRAIGHT

We normally use the Lasso tool for drawing freeform selections, but you'll find that oftentimes, while drawing your selection, you'll need to draw a perfectly straight segment, even for just a few pixels. You can do just that by holding the Option key (PC: Alt key), releasing the mouse button, and continuing to draw your selection. You'll notice that your cursor changes to the Polygonal Lasso tool and that as you move the mouse, a perfectly straight selection will drag out. When you've dragged the straight selection where you want, click-and-hold the mouse button (to add a point), release the Option/Alt key, and you'll be back to the regular Lasso tool again. Drag the mouse to continue drawing your selection.

   SKIP THE ZOOM TOOL

The Zoom tool is okay to use when you need to zoom in on a particular area, but if you need to zoom out, it stinks. That's because you have to hold the Option key (PC: Alt key) and click on your image, and every time you do, it only zooms outward one step. Want to zoom in and out of your image like a pro? Instead press Command-+ (PC: Control-+) to quickly zoom in, and Command--- (PC: Control---) to zoom out (that's the minus key for zooming out). Start using this, and you'll only grab the Zoom tool to zoom in, and then only half as much as you used to.

CAN'T REMEMBER SELECTION SHORTCUTS? LOOK AT THE CURSOR

If you've made a selection and want to add to that selection, just hold the Shift key and you can add more area to it. Of course, we just told you it was the Shift key, but what if you couldn't remember which key it was? Just press a modifier key (such as Shift, Option/Alt, Command/Control, etc.) then look at your cursor. When you hold the Shift key, a little plus sign appears at the bottom right-hand corner of the cursor to tell you that you can now add to the selection. Hold Option (PC: Alt) and a minus sign appears to tell you that you can now subtract from the selection. Hold Command (PC: Control) and a pair of scissors appears, telling you that if you click-and-drag the selection, it will cut out the image inside of the selection and move it right along with the cursor.

   SNAP YOUR PALETTES TO ORDER

If you like order in your world, then you'll love this tip for making your palettes snap to the edge of your screen. Just hold the Shift key and click on the topmost bar of your palette and it will snap to the closest edge (left, right, top, or bottom), bringing order and harmony to your workspace once again. Ahhhhh.

YOUR SELECTIONS AREN'T STUCK—MOVE 'EM!

If you've drawn a selection and it didn't quite wind up in the exact spot you wanted, you can move it. The key is making sure you move it with a Selection tool (Lasso, Rectangular Marquee, Magic Wand, etc.), rather than the Move tool. Just move your cursor inside your selected area and you'll notice that it changes to a hollow arrow with a square selection. That's letting you know you're just moving the selection, so now you can drag the selection wherever you want. You can also use the Arrow keys on your keyboard to nudge your selection around if you prefer. If you switch to the Move tool and move the selection, it will move the pixels under your selection, rather than moving the selection itself.

   ONE-BUTTON REFRESH FOR THE FILE BROWSER

When you're ranking images in Photoshop CS's File Browser, you've probably noticed that the sorting (by rank) doesn't happen automatically as you rank each image—you have to either change your "Sort By" pop-up menu at the bottom of the File Browser to a different choice (like Filename) and then switch back to Rank, or you have to choose Refresh Desktop View from the File Browser's pop-down menu. Either way, unless you're charging by the hour, it just takes too long. Instead, just press F5 for an instant refresh anytime.

GET RID OF THE ANNOYING CHECKERBOARD PATTERN

Any time you create a new layer, by default Photoshop puts a checkerboard pattern behind the transparent areas of your layer. The idea is so that you'll know which areas are transparent. We've always felt we had something that would tell us which areas were transparent—our eyes. So we (and many other users) turned this annoying checkerboard off as soon as we learned how. Here's how: In Mac OS X, go under the Photoshop menu, under Preferences, and choose Transparency & Gamut (in Windows, Preferences can be found under the Edit menu). In the dialog, change the Grid Size from Medium to None. That's it—click OK and the annoying grid is gone. (Want to play a Photoshop prank? Go to a friend's or coworker's computer and change their Grid Size to Large and the Grid Colors to Dark. If that doesn't send them into rehab, nothing will.)

   UNDERSTANDING THE GIANT MONDO-BIG BRUSHES PALETTE

If you're freaked out by all the sliders, menus, buttons, and clutter in the new expanded (read incredibly huge behemoth) Brushes palette, I have a tip that will help you to understand how it works so that it will immediately feel more friendly and familiar. Here it is: It works much the same way as the Layer Styles dialog. That's right. If you look at the Layer Styles dialog, the menu on the left side of it looks, and works, pretty much like the left-side menu in the expanded Brushes palette. For example, in the Layer Styles dialog, to add an effect, you click on the check-box, but to edit that effect's options, you click on its name. This is the same in the Brushes palette. To add an effect to your current brush, click on the checkbox beside the effect. To edit that effect, click directly on the effect's name, and its options appear.

HOW TO TAME THE SELECT SIMILAR COMMAND

A popular trick for making selections of large areas (such as backgrounds) is to select part of the background that contains most of the colors that appear within that background. Then you can go under the Select menu and choose Similar. Photoshop will then select all the similar colors in your image. This can really speed up the task of selecting an entire background, especially if the background is limited to just a few colors. Here's the tip: Do you know what determines how many pixels out the Similar command selects? Believe it or not, it's controlled by the Magic Wand's Tolerance setting. The higher the setting, the more pixels it selects. Eerie, ain't it? Sooooooo… if you use Similar, and it doesn't select enough colors, go to the Magic Wand tool, increase the Tolerance setting, and then try running Similar again. This all makes perfect sense (at least to an engineer at Adobe).

 RUN THAT FILTER ONE MORE TIME

Once you've applied a filter to your image, Photoshop thoughtfully puts that filter at the top of the list in your Filter menu, just in case you decide to run that exact same filter again, with the exact same settings. That way, you don't have to go digging through your Filter submenus tracking it down to run it again. However, even more convenient is the keyboard shortcut that lets you run it again without going to the Filter menu at all. It's Command-F (PC: Control-F). What if you don't want the same settings (ahhh, I knew you were going to ask that)? Try pressing Command-Option-F (PC: Control-Alt-F), which brings up the dialog for the last filter you applied with the last settings that you used.

DON'T LET THE BROWSER PREVIEW FOOL YOU

When you rotate an image in the File Browser, Photoshop doesn't actually rotate the file until you open the image, so all you're really rotating is the preview. If you want the image permanently rotated, you have to open the image, let Photoshop rotate it, and then resave it. Only then will the image become permanently

rotated. Otherwise, you're just telling Photoshop, "Hey, when you open this image, rotate it for me, okay?" It just saves you a step.

  ## WANT THE DEFAULT COLORS? JUST "D-DO" IT

Photoshop's default setting for the Foreground color is black, and the default for the Background color is white. There's a tiny little icon below and to the left of your Foreground/Background swatches in the Toolbox that lets you return to those defaults anytime by clicking on it, but there's actually a faster way than making the trip to the Toolbox—just press the letter "d" on your keyboard.

SCRUBBY SLIDER SHIFT-CLICK TRICK

Adobe borrowed scrubby sliders, a very cool feature from Adobe After Effects, and put it in Photoshop CS. You use it by clicking on a field's name, rather than in the field itself, and the value in the field changes as you drag (scrub) over the field's name. However, it scrubs in very small increments. That is, unless you hold the Shift key, which is ideal when you need to make big changes in the field (like from 0 to 256).

   SAVING TIME IN THE FILL DIALOG

For as long as there's been a Photoshop, whenever you open the Fill dialog from the Edit menu, you'd better have your Foreground color set to the Fill color you want, or you'd have to hit Cancel, choose a new Foreground color, then open Fill again. Sadly, I did this same "Open fill, hit Cancel, choose new color, open fill again" routine literally hundreds of times. But no more my friends, because now, at long last, in the Fill dialog's Use pop-down menu there is a menu command for Color, which brings up the Color Picker while you're in the Fill dialog. Life as we know it will never be the same.

WHY THE FILE BROWSER WON'T DOCK

If you're used to docking the File Browser up in the Options Bar's Palette Well, you're going to have to get used to not docking it there in Photoshop CS. Ever. Even though it was docked there by default back in Photoshop 7, you can't put it there anymore. That's because it's do darn big. It's gargantuan. In fact, that's probably why Adobe says that Photoshop CS only supports resolutions greater than 800x600. Adobe put the new File Browser button to the immediate left of the Palette Well, so if you're used to looking for the Browser in the Palette Well, you'll find it right nearby.

Tool Presets

   ESCAPE FROM THE CROP TOOL (OR DIE!)

Sometimes when you're using the Crop tool, you change your mind and decide not to crop. If this happens to you, do you have to crop and then press the Undo shortcut? Nah, press the Escape key to cancel your crop and remove the cropping border. You can also click on the "⊘" icon on the far right of the Options Bar to cancel a crop as well. Okay, there's one more way, just switch tools—a dialog will appear asking you if you want to complete the crop or not. Just hit Don't Crop.

GETTING THE STARTUP WINDOW BACK

When you first launch Photoshop CS, it brings up a Welcome Screen that has links to tutorials, a list of what's new, etc. There's also a checkbox at the bottom called Show this Dialog at Startup that you'll probably uncheck before too long, because after a short while the Welcome Screen tends to get on your nerves (that's why Adobe put that checkbox there in the first place). However, if you've checked that "hide the welcome screen" box, and then one day you have some extra time and you'd like to explore what the Welcome Screen has to offer, you can temporarily bring it back by going under the Help menu and choosing Welcome Screen.

   GETTING YOUR WARNINGS BACK (RESETTING ALL DIALOGS)

One thing I love about Photoshop is that a number of warning dialogs have a magical checkbox that says "Don't show this dialog again" (or something along those lines). However, if you later decide you want these warning dialogs put back into play (this is especially helpful if you're training someone new on your computer), you can have them become active again. Just go under the Photoshop menu (PC: Edit menu), under Preferences, and choose General Preferences. In the General Preferences dialog, click on the button at the bottom of the panel named Reset All Warning Dialogs.

HOW TO SEE YOUR VECTOR EPS FILES IN THE FILE BROWSER

Back in Photoshop 7, if you had a vector EPS file (like
an EPS file from Adobe Illustrator) the File Browser
basically ignored it. But in Photoshop CS, you can
see, and even open these vector EPS files as Photoshop raster files, but to do that, you have to make
a little change in the Preferences. Go under the File
Browser's Edit menu and choose Preferences. In the
Options section at the bottom of the dialog, click on the Render Vector Files checkbox.

   ## THE SMALLER TOOLBOX TRICK

Is that Toolbox taking up too much space, but you don't want to close it,
because a few seconds later, sure enough, you'll need a tool? Then just
double-click on the very top of your Toolbox and it will tuck up out of the
way, leaving just that little tab showing. Need it back fast, just double-click the little
tab again and it comes right back.

BRUSHES PALETTE: THAT'S NOT A HEADER, IT'S A BUTTON

If you look in the expanded Brushes palette, there's a list of controls on the left side of the dialog. At the top it reads "Brush Presets," and you might figure that you can click on that and get some options, but the one that catches just about everyone off guard is just below that. It's the header for "Brush Tip Shape." It appears to be a header for a list of brush tip options below it, but in reality, it's a button (I know, it doesn't look like a button, but it is). Click right on the words "Brush Tip Shape" and the Brush Tip Shape options are revealed in the main panel.

   DANGEROUS INTERSECTION?

You've already learned that if you're using a selection tool (Lasso, Rectangular Marquee, etc.) and you need to add an additional area to your currently selected area, you can hold the Shift key, then any selection you draw with one of those tools will be added. But what if you have a selection and instead you want to create a new selection that will intersect with your existing selection to create an entirely new selection (Whew! That sounds complicated just explaining it)? Here's how: Draw your first selection, then up in the Options Bar you'll find four icons for various selection options. The fourth icon is called "Intersect with Selection." Click on it, then draw another selection that overlaps your existing selection and all will become clear (grasshopper).

NUDGING POWER

As you know, as long as you have the Move tool selected, you can move (or nudge) your current layer using the Up/Down/Left/Right Arrow keys on your keyboard. For every press of an Arrow, it nudges your layer 1 pixel in that direction. However, if you hold the Shift key and use the Arrow keys, it nudges the object 10 pixels at a time.

   MAKE THAT OPTIONS BAR FLOAT— FLOAT???

You may not realize it, but the Options Bar, which seems permanently docked to the top of your work area, can actually be redocked to the bottom of your screen, or you can make it into a floating palette. To make it float, just click on the little tab on the far left side of the bar and drag it away and voilà, it floats. To dock it at the bottom of your screen, drag the tab down to the bottom left-hand side of your screen and it snaps into place. You can even hide the Options Bar altogether by choosing "Options" from the Window menu. You can always get it back by double-clicking on any tool.

WHERE'S THE 3D TRANSFORM FILTER?

You can kill a lot of otherwise productive time searching for the 3D Transform filter that's been in Photoshop for years. That's because—it ain't there. It no longer installs when you install Photoshop CS, but Adobe thought that somebody, somewhere, might want to use it for something, so even though it doesn't install, you can find it in the Goodies folder on the Photoshop CS Install disc. Just drag it into Photoshop's Filters folder inside the Plug-ins folder to get it back in your Filter menu.

   ## THE FATE OF CLIPPING GROUPS

If you're looking under the Layer menu and can't find the familiar command for Clipping Group, don't sweat it. It's still there; Adobe just changed the name. In Photoshop CS, Clipping Groups are now called Clipping Masks (which are really more descriptive of what they are).

SUPERSIZE IT

This is a super speed trick for getting your image view up (or down) to size. To instantly view your image at 100% size, double-click on the Zoom tool in the Toolbox. To have your image fit as large as possible on your screen (called "Fit On Screen"), double-click the Hand tool.

   LOCK THOSE PIXELS AND FILL

This is a great timesaving shortcut when you have an object on a layer and you want to fill just the object with the Foreground color (rather than filling the entire layer with color). Press Shift-Option-Delete (PC: Shift-Alt-Backspace). What this does is turn on Lock Transparent Pixels for the layer in the Layers palette, fills the object on your layer, and then turns Lock Transparent Pixels back off. What if you want to fill your object with a gradient? It's a little more laborious. Turn on Lock Transparent Pixels by using the Forward Slash key (/) shortcut. Drag your Gradient tool through your object, and then press Forward Slash (/) again to turn off Lock Transparent Pixels.

STEAL COLOR FROM ANYWHERE

In previous versions of Photoshop, you could click the Eyedropper tool on any color within your image, and it would steal that color and make it your new Foreground color. The only drawback was, you could only steal colors from within an open document window. Back in Photoshop 7.0, Adobe cut the Eyedropper tool loose from the chains that bound it, and now, as long as you click within an open image first, you can drag right out of your image window and sample a color from, well, anywhere. That includes sampling colors from other

applications, Photoshop's own Toolbox and menu bars, and even your computer's desktop pattern. Just remember to click in your image first, and then drag that Eyedropper to a new world of color delights that dare not speak its name.

   ASK PHOTOSHOP TO REMEMBER MORE

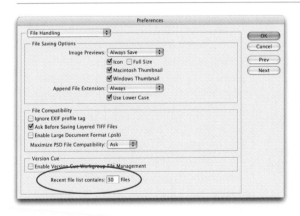

Photoshop CS remembers the last 30 documents that you had open, but by default it only displays the last four under the File menu, under Open Recent. However, you're not limited to just four. Would you rather Photoshop displayed the last eight instead? Then in Mac OS X, go under the Photoshop menu, under Preferences, and choose File Handling (in Windows, Prefer-ences can be found under the Edit menu). When the dialog appears, under "Recent File List Contains," enter the desired number of files (up to 30) that you want to have quick access to under the Open Recent menu.

THE MONDO-COOL BATCH RANKING SECRET SHORTCUT

If you're using Photoshop CS's File Browser, you're probably already using the handy ranking system, where you can sort your images by ranking the best images, then the second best, third best, etc. If you have a lot of images, this can really take some time, but if you use this cool hidden little tip (shown to me by Adobe's own graphics evangelist and undisputed Queen of Photoshop, Julieanne Kost), you can

make quick work of it (whatever that means). Here's how: Open the File Browser, and then Command-click on all the images you want to share a similar rank (like all the best images in a particular folder of images). Then, Control-click (PC: Right-click) in one of those Command-clicked images and a pop-up menu will appear, and when you choose a ranking for this one image, all the Command-clicked images will automatically share the same ranking, saving you a boatload of time (which frankly is a time measurement that is vastly underused).

   SHRINK THOSE PALETTES DOWN TO SIZE

Are your palettes in the way, but you don't want to hide them all using the Tab key? You can double-click the palette's name tab, and the palette will minimize down to just the tab itself, giving you back lots of screen real estate. Need the palette back, just double-click on its tab again.

STOP THE WARNINGS FROM YOUR DIGITAL CAMERA IMAGES

Many digital cameras embed the sRGB color space into their photos, but most photographers choose to use Adobe RGB (1998) as their Photoshop

color space instead. Because of this "mismatch," every time you open a photo from your camera, you get a "mismatch" warning, and that can get really old. Luckily, Adobe felt your pain, and in Photoshop CS there's a way to have Photoshop globally ignore the embedded sRGB profile in your digital camera images, thereby alleviating the warning dialog. Just go under the Photoshop menu (PC: Edit menu), under Preferences, and choose File Handling. In the File Handling Preferences, turn on the checkbox for Ignore EXIF Profile Tag, and the sRGB tag will be ignored.

   CREATING THE ÜBER PALETTE

You've been able to nest one or more palettes into another palette since back in Photoshop 3.0. No big deal, but now you can not only nest but you can also dock palettes one atop the other, creating a giant über palette. Here's how: Drag the name tab of one palette to the bottom edge of a second palette and slowly drag upward. A thin, black double-line will appear at the bottom of the top palette, letting you know it's "time to dock." Release the mouse and your palettes will be docked, one on top of the other. Now, when you move the top palette, all docked palettes will move with it as a group. We use this feature to stack our Character and Paragraph palettes so we can access all our type settings in one place.

KILLING LAYERS WITH NO MERCY

Want to delete a layer with as much speed and prejudice as possible? Try this: Hold the Option key (PC: Alt key) and click on the Trash icon at the bottom of the Layers palette. Bang—it's gone. No warning dialog, no muss, no fuss. If you hold Shift-Option-Esc-F13-Control-Delete-Page Up, it will even drive the layer out to the docks and dump it in the East River.

   TIRED OF PRESSING THE SHIFT KEY TO ROTATE THROUGH TOOLS?

Back in the old days, there just weren't that many tools in Photoshop, and if you wanted to rotate through the various tools (say the Pen tool for instance), you'd just press the letter "p" over and over again until the Pen tool you wanted made its way to the Toolbox. Ah, those were simpler times. But as Photoshop 5.0, 5.5, 6.0, 7.0 and now CS came about, so did more tools, and now by default you also have to press Shift to rotate through the tools. Or do you?

Hmmmm. Actually, you can request (politely) that Photoshop let you revert to the ways of old, allowing you to press just one key to rotate through the tools. You do this in Mac OS X by going under the Photoshop menu, under Preferences, and choosing General (in Windows, Preferences can be found under the Edit menu). In that dialog, uncheck the box for "Use Shift Key for Tool Switch." It's like stepping back in time.

FIX THOSE TOOL SETTINGS FAST

There's no doubt you'll be "messing" with many, if not all, of the options for the tools you use every day in Photoshop. One day you'll go to use a tool, and you'll have messed with it to the extent that something's just not right. To quickly get back to any tool's default settings, choose the tool from the Toolbox, then Control-click (PC: Right-click) on the tool's icon that appears up in the Options Bar at the far left. A pop-up menu will appear where you can choose Reset Tool to set it back to its factory-fresh defaults. By the way, while you're there, you can also choose Reset All Tools and they will all revert to their defaults as well.

BRING ORDER BACK TO YOUR WORLD

In Photoshop, you're constantly moving your palettes around, and before long, you've got one messy set of palettes littering your screen. If your palettes get messy, you're only one simple menu command from having them back at their factory-fresh default locations. Just go under the Window menu, under Workspace, and choose Reset Palette Locations, and all will be right with your world once again (that is, until you mess 'em up again).

THE UNDOCUMENTED FILL SHORTCUT

There are all sorts of keyboard shortcuts for filling selections, entire layers, and stuff like that, but if you look under the Edit menu, next to the Fill command, there doesn't appear to be a shortcut for bringing up the Fill dialog itself. Luckily, there's an undocumented keyboard shortcut that will do the trick—it's Shift-Delete (PC: Shift-Backspace). This is a good one to pull on your Photoshop buddies and coworkers as a Photoshop trivia question, because few people know it exists.

  ## DESELECTED AND FORGOT TO SAVE? DON'T SWEAT IT

If, after you've created a selection in an image, deselected it, and moved on to other things, you suddenly wish you had that selection back, you're not out of luck. As long as you haven't made another selection (since the one you want to get back), Photoshop remembers your last selection and lets you get it back by going under the Select menu and choosing Reselect. When you choose it, the last selection you created reappears within your image. If you create a selection that, while it's still active, you know you want to keep for later use, then go under the Select menu and choose Save Selection. When the Save Selection dialog appears, click OK, and Photoshop saves it. You can reload it anytime by going under the Select menu and choosing Load Selection. Your selection will be named "Alpha 1" by default, and you can choose to load it (or other subsequent saved selections) from the pop-up menu in the Load Selection dialog.

SUPER-FAST INCHES TO PIXELS

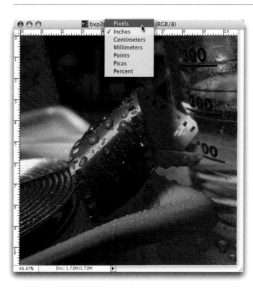

Want to change the unit of measurement for your image? Don't go digging through Photoshop's menus for the Preferences dialog; just Control-click (PC: Right-click) on Photoshop's rulers, and a pop-up menu will appear with a list of measurement units. Choose the one you want, and your rulers will instantly reflect the change. If you feel you must access the Units & Rulers Preferences dialog, just double-click anywhere on one of Photoshop's rulers and the dialog will appear.

   LIGHTNING-FAST FEATHER

If you're using the Lasso tool and want to add a feather to soften the edges of the selection, there's no faster way than this: Hit the Return key (PC: Enter key) and the Feather field in the Options Bar will highlight. Then all you have to do is enter the value for how much feathering you want (just remember to set the feathering back to zero when you're done, using the same shortcut).

BOSS AROUND YOUR COLOR SWATCHES

Here are a few tips for using the Swatches palette. I'm sure you know that if you click on a color in the Swatches palette, that color becomes your new Foreground color. Here's one you may not have realized—if you Command-click (PC: Control-click) on a swatch, that color now becomes your Background color. Also, you can delete any swatch by holding the Option key (PC: Alt key) and clicking on the swatch you want to remove. You can also add a color to your swatches by setting your Foreground color to the color you want to save, then holding the Shift key and clicking on any open space in the Swatches palette.

   ZOOMED IN? DON'T USE THE SCROLL BARS

If you've zoomed in on an image, using the scroll bars can be incredibly frustrating, because you move just a tiny bit. Here's how to get around that—don't use the scroll bars. (Okay, there's more to it than that.) Instead, when you're zoomed in, use the Hand tool, but to save time, access it by simply pressing the Spacebar. It temporarily switches you to the Hand, letting you easily navigate through your zoomed image.

LET PHOTOSHOP DO THE MATH WHEN COPYING/PASTING

If you've selected something within your Photoshop document and you want to copy and paste that item into its own separate document, don't worry about typing the Width and Height into Photoshop's New document dialog. Photoshop automatically figures that you're going to paste that image into a new document, so when you open the New dialog, the exact size of your copied selection has already been entered for you, so just click OK, and then paste your image inside—it'll be a perfect fit.

INSTANT SELECTION FROM ANY PATH

When you're using the Pen tool to create a path, you can go to the Paths palette and click on the third icon from the left (at the bottom of the palette) to turn your path into a selection, or you can use the keyboard shortcut Command-Return (PC: Control-Enter). We prefer the keyboard shortcut, because it will do the exact same job faster and saves us from opening the Paths palette, taking up valuable screen real estate.

MAXIMUM FILE BROWSER HIDDEN SHORTCUT

There's a little hidden Photoshop CS shortcut that lets you open the File Browser in Full Screen Mode with Menu Bar, and it even hides the Toolbox and palettes for you, giving you the maximum amount of viewing space. Just

hold the Command key (PC: Control key), and then click on the File Browser button up in the Options Bar, and you'll get the maximum view File Browser. Closing the File Browser won't get your palettes back—you have to Command-click (PC: Control-click) the File Browser button again. To get back to the regular setup (the standard size File Browser and all your palettes back) just click the Browser's Zoom button, then press the Tab key on your keyboard twice.

   ## CANVAS COLOR QUICK CHANGE

In previous versions of Photoshop, before you went to the Canvas Size dialog you had to choose your Background color first, and if you didn't have it set to white, you'd have to do the old "cancel Canvas Size, set your Background color, go back to Canvas Size" routine. It was brutal. Luckily, in Photoshop CS you can now choose your canvas color from right within the Canvas Size dialog. If you want a white canvas (which is the most common choice) you can choose it directly from the pop-up menu at the bottom. If you want a different color, just click on the Color Swatch.

SAVE CLICKS WHEN YOU CLOSE

This is such a quick little tip that you might not think that it matters, but it saves a few seconds every time you close a document. If you close a number of documents a day (and my guess is, you do), it really starts to add up fast. When you close a document, Photoshop presents you with a dialog asking, "Save changes to the Adobe Photoshop document before closing?" You have three choices: (1) Don't Save, (2) Cancel, and (3) Save. Here's the shortcut: Press the letter "d" for Don't Save, press "s" for Save, and "c" for Cancel.

   ## BEEN BINGING ON RAM? MAYBE IT'S TIME TO PURGE!

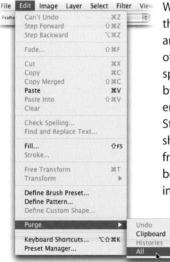

What do you do if the dreaded "Not enough RAM to complete this function" dialog appears? Outside of buying more RAM and installing it on the spot, you might want to purge some of the "junk" hanging around in RAM so you can free up some space to complete the project you're working on. You do this by going under the Edit menu, under Purge, and choosing to empty either your Undo, Photoshop's Clipboard, your History States, or everything at once (All). They're in the order you should proceed, so first try purging your Undo and see if that frees up enough memory. If that doesn't do it, try the Clipboard, then Histories. If that doesn't do it, try this super-slick insider tip: Make a tiny (1x1″) selection within your document, and then go under the Edit menu and choose Copy three times in a row. Believe it or not, it often works, and has gotten us out of more than one sticky situation.

REACHING THE FREE TRANSFORM HANDLES

If you want to use Free Transform on a layer, but your image extends beyond the edges of your document window (and this happens frequently if you're collaging different photos together), you won't be able to reach the Free Transform handles to scale your image down to size. Here's the hidden keyboard shortcut that lets you reach each and every handle, no matter how far the image extends outside your current canvas area. Just press Command-T (PC: Control-T) to bring up Free Transform, then press Command-0 (PC: Control-0), and your window will zoom out to exactly the right size to enable you to reach all the handles. Cool!

   TRANSFORMING AND COPYING AT THE SAME TIME

Generally, when you apply a transformation to an object (scaling, rotating, distorting, perspective), you apply that transformation to the object itself. However, here's a cool tip if you want to apply a transformation (using Free Transform) on a duplicate of your object, rather than on the original: Press Option-Command-T (PC: Alt-Control-T), then use the Free Transform tool as you usually would. You'll notice that as you begin to transform, the original object remains untouched, and a copy is transformed instead.

Greased Lightnin'

COOL TIPS

Why is this chapter named "Way Cool Tips"? It's because "Boring Regular Tips" was already taken (psyche!). Actually, it's because this is where a lot of the

Greased Lightnin'

way cool tips

really cool tips wound up that didn't fit into any of the other categories. I don't really have anything else to say about this chapter, so instead, let's fill this space by singing a verse of "Greased Lightnin'" from the motion picture Grease.

"We'll get some overhead lifters, and four-barrel quads, oh yeah (keep talkin', whoa, keep talkin'). Fuel-injection cutoff and chrome-plated rods, oh yeah (I'll get the money, I'll see you get the money), with the four-speed on the floor, they'll be waitin' at the door, you know that ain't no…" Hey, wait a minute—that next word is a cuss word. Okay, no problem, we'll skip over that word and continue, "…we'll be getting lots of…." Geez, another nasty word. I've been singing that song for years and never really noticed how nasty it was. Just to be safe, let's just jump to the end of the chorus, "…you know that I ain't braggin', she's a real…." Oh, that's just wrong! I'm stopping right here.

THE TRICK TO TRICKY EXTRACTIONS

Adobe's own Julieanne Kost (Photoshop guru and instructor supreme) showed this last year at the PhotoshopWorld Conference & Expo (before Photoshop CS was announced), and it had everybody's jaw dropping, but little has been said of it since, even though it's built into Photoshop CS's Extract function (found under the Filter menu). It's called Textured Image and you use it when you're dealing with a tough extraction—a person with a dark shirt posing on a dark background, for example—and Extract can't really tell where the shirt ends and the background begins. Turning this on helps detect the edges by examining the texture, and if it detects a texture (like you might find in a shirt), it can often help pull you out of a tight situation.

   LIVE PATCHING PREVIEW

I always preferred the Patch tool to its cousin the Healing Brush because I always felt it let me get more retouching done in less time, but you never knew if the area you were using as your source was going to work well for your selected repair area. But in Photoshop CS, you can look inside your originally selected area as you drag the selection to a clean area, and see a preview of that area to give you a better idea of just how that repair is going to look before you release the mouse.

ZOOMING ALL YOUR TILED IMAGES AT ONCE

If you've chosen to tile your open windows (in the Window menu, under Arrange, choose Tile), in Photoshop CS you get some hidden functionality. If you want all the tiled images to be displayed at the same level of magnification, just hold the Shift key, grab the Zoom tool, zoom in on one of the images, and all the other tiled images will jump to that same magnification. This is great when you're trying to compare a number of similar images for detail.

FINDING THE PHOTOGRAPHIC BRUSH TIPS

Adobe hid 'em, but they're there—a few photographic brush tips, and it's worth giving them a try just to see what they can do. To find these photographic brush tips, go to the Brushes palette, and from the palette's pop-down menu, load the set named Special Effect Brushes. Try the Large Roses brush (just click it a couple of times in your image), or the Ducks brush. Then click-and-drag the first brush (the flowers) and watch what happens. Try the third brush in the list, and paint a few strokes. Pretty neat stuff.

HOW TO DUPLICATE A COLOR STOP

Here's the scenario: You're making a custom gradient and you need to duplicate one or more of the Color Stops. No problem. Once you've created one gradient Color Stop, you can make copies by Option-dragging it (PC: Alt-dragging). Also, as long as you keep the Option key (PC: Alt key) down while you drag, you can jump right over other existing Stops. It's a Color Stop love fest. Can you feel it?

   REMOVING EDGE FRINGE WHEN COLLAGING

Any time you're creating a collage, you'll eventually add an image that has little white pixels around the edges of your object. Here's a tip for getting rid of that "fringe." Go under the Layer menu, under Matting, and choose Defringe. Try the default setting of 1 pixel and click OK. What this does (here's the techno speak) is replace the edge pixels with a combination of the pixel colors in your object and the colors in the background (whew, that hurt). That usually does the trick. If it doesn't, Undo it, then try a 2- or 3-pixel Defringe.

CRACKING THE EASTER EGG MYSTERY

Easter Eggs are usually funny little messages hidden within an application (engineer humor just cracks us up). Photoshop has a few of its own, but one of the lesser-known Easter Eggs is "Merlin Lives." To see this Easter Egg, go to the Paths palette, hold the Option key (PC: Alt key), and in the palette's pop-down menu, choose Palette Options. When you do, a tiny floating palette will appear with a picture of Merlin and just one button named "Begone," which closes the dialog. I have to party with those engineer guys .

   SUPERCHARGE YOUR FILTER EFFECTS

Next time before you apply a cool filter to an image, instead of just selecting an area and applying the filter, press Command-J (PC: Control-J) to put your selected area up on its own layer. What's the advantage of this? Well first, it gives you more control over the effect. For example, by having the area on its own layer, after you apply the filter, you can then change the Blend Modes of the layer to get even more out of the filters (multiplying it, screening it, overlaying it, etc.). And secondly, you have control of your filter "after the fact." If, after you apply the filter, you feel it's too intense, you can always lower the Opacity of the layer to calm it down a bit.

UNDO ON A SLIDER!

If you apply a technique (such as a filter or a paint stroke) and the effect is too intense, you can always undo the effect by pressing Command-Z (PC: Control-Z). But if you just want to decrease the intensity, instead of completely undoing it, go under Edit, and choose Fade. Want a less intense effect? Just move the slider to the left. The farther you drag, the less intense the effect. Drag all the way to the left, and the effect is undone.

   GETTING TO THE FOLDER OF PHOTOS YOU WANT—FAST!

Tired of trying to navigate your entire drive using that tiny navigation window in the File Browser? What if you could instantly jump right to the folder of images you want? Well, in Photoshop CS it's easy. If you can see the folder on your hard drive, you're set—just drag that folder from your desktop (or wherever it is on your hard drive) and either drop

it right on the drop-down menu at the top of the File Browser or on the Preview palette on the left-hand side. The File Browser will immediately target that folder as the current folder. Now, here's the catch: You can't just drag this folder anywhere in the File Browser window—it only works if you drag the folder directly to that pop-up menu or the Preview palette (they will highlight when you're right over either one of them).

TWO FILES ARE BETTER THAN ONE

There are times when we should be working (or experimenting) on a copy of an image—it's a shame to trash a good image and then try to recreate it. You could always do a Save As and choose As a Copy, but here's a better way: Go to the bottom of the History palette and click on the Create New Snapshot icon (the one that looks like a camera). Click on the new snapshot near the top of the History palette to make it the active History state. Finally, go to the bottom of the History palette and click on the Create New Document from Current State icon. There you go, a copy of the image, just dying for you to trash it.

RESIZING PATHS THE EASY WAY

When you're using the Pen tool, you can visually resize your path by using the Path Selection tool. To do this, go up in the Options Bar and turn on the checkbox for Show Bounding Box. This puts a Free Transform-like bounding box around your path, and you can use this bounding box to resize your path by dragging the handles (remember to hold the Shift key to resize it proportionately).

THE GAUSSIAN BLUR KEYBOARD SHORTCUT

I thought that would get your attention. That's because you know there's no keyboard shortcut for applying a Gaussian Blur. But there is in my copy of Photoshop CS. How is that possible? Because I created one, and you can too. Just go under the Edit menu and choose Keyboard Shortcuts to bring up the Keyboard Shortcuts editor. Then, from the Shortcuts For pop-up menu, choose Application Menus. In the list of menus in the window beneath it, click on the gray, right-facing triangle next to Filter to reveal all the choices under the Filter menu. Scroll down to Gaussian Blur, then click on the name. This brings up a field where you can enter the shortcut by pressing the keys you want to use. I recommend using Shift-Option-Command-G (PC: Shift-Alt-Control-G) because there are so few shortcuts not already being used by Photoshop. Click OK, and not only is the shortcut activated but your custom shortcut now appears in the Filter menu to the right of Gaussian Blur.

   THE ADVANTAGE OF PHOTO FILTER ADJUSTMENT LAYERS

One of the most brilliant things Adobe did when they added Photo Filters to Photoshop CS (these filters replicate the old traditional screw-on lens filters) was to make them Adjustment Layers. By doing this, after you apply the Photo Filter (let's say, for example, you used the 81 filter to warm a cool photo), you can get the Brush tool, set your Foreground color to black, and paint over any areas of the photo you don't want to be warmed. This gives you a level of flexibility you wouldn't get any other way.

WHERE TO SET CUSTOM VIEW SIZES

Although you can choose Custom Thumbnail Size from the File Browser's View menu, that custom size is set by Adobe to 256 pixels. But if it says "custom," surely you have to be able to customize it, right? Right! Just go under the File Browser's Edit menu and choose Preferences. When the Preferences dialog appears, you'll see a field for Custom Thumbnail Size. Highlight this field, enter your new default size, and click OK. Now when you choose Custom Thumbnail Size from the View menu, it will use your size (rather than the old default).

   MOVING YOUR IMAGE IN FULL SCREEN MODE

In Photoshop CS you can pull off something users have been wanting for years—the ability to change the placement of your entire image once you're in Full Screen Mode (where your image is centered on screen, surrounded by a black border with no menus, palettes, or tools visible). Just enter Full Screen Mode (press f, f, then Tab), hold the Spacebar, and your cursor will change into the Hand tool. Click-and-drag your entire image anywhere on the screen you'd like. To return to regular mode, press f then Tab.

DON'T RANK IT—FLAG IT

I have to admit it—ranking in Photoshop 7's File Browser was a bit clunky. You had to Control-click (PC: Right-click) on a file then choose a ranking of A, B, C, or D for each photo. In Photoshop CS, the process of sorting the "keepers" from the "dumpers" has gotten much more streamlined thanks to flagging. As you search through your photos in the File Browser, when you come to one you want to keep (a "keeper") just press Command-' (PC: Control-' [that's an apostrophe]) and the file becomes "flagged" (it even adds a tiny flag icon to the bottom right corner of the photo's thumbnail). Once you're done flagging, to see just your flagged photos, from the Show pop-up menu (in the upper right-hand corner of the File Browser) choose Flagged Files.

   PHOTO-RETOUCHING SAFETY TIP

Here's a tip that many photo retouchers use—do all your retouching on a layer above your image. That way, you don't damage the underlying image, and you have control over Opacity and Blend Modes you normally wouldn't have. It's also easy to erase areas you wish you hadn't retouched. The key to making this work is to click on the Clone Stamp tool and in the Options Bar, turn on the Use All Layers option. That way you can sample from the underlying image and then paint on the layer above it (believe it or not, by default Photoshop doesn't let you do that—it only lets you clone from the active layer to that same layer).

PHOTOSHOP'S HIDDEN STEP AND REPEAT

Although Photoshop doesn't have a visible Step and Repeat function (like many vector or page layout programs do), it still has the feature—it's just a bit hidden. For example, let's say you have an object on a layer, and you want to duplicate and move or rotate that object a number of times in succession (a typical step-and-repeat), here's how you can do it in Photoshop CS: Start by going to the original layer with the object, then press Option-Command-T (PC: Alt-Control-T) to bring up a special version of Free Transform. Now you can transform your object (move it, rotate it, skew it, etc.) then press Return (PC: Enter) to lock in your transformation. You'll notice that your original object remains untouched on its layer and you now have a new layer with the transformed object. Now press Shift-Option-Command-T (PC: Shift-Alt-Control-T) and this will create a duplicate of your last move, and at the same time it creates a new layer, thereby giving you a step and repeat (you have to try this once, and you'll immediately "get it").

   PAUSING FOR A BRUSH PREVIEW

If you're choosing your brush tips from the expanded Brushes palette, you don't have to actually click on a brush to see the large preview of it at the bottom of the Brushes palette. Instead, just pause your cursor right over the brush you want to preview, and in just a second the preview will appear, even though you didn't actually click on the brush tip. The catch is: Tool Tips must be turned on in the General Preferences for this "pause preview" to work.

THE UNDOCUMENTED AIRBRUSH TOGGLE TRICK

This cool, undocumented shortcut comes from our good friend, Web wizard, and all-powerful overlord of every Photoshop keyboard shortcut known to man, Michael Ninness (author of the book *Photoshop 7 Power Shortcuts*, from New Riders, ISBN 0735713316). Here's the tip: As you probably know by now, the Airbrush tool has been gone from the Toolbox since 7.0, but you can add Airbrush control to the brush tools by clicking on the Airbrush icon found in the Options Bar of each Brush tool (with the exception of the Blur and Sharpen tools—don't ask me why). However, that takes a lot of trips up to the Options Bar. Ah, if only there were a keyboard shortcut that would let you toggle this Airbrush feature on and off at will. Well, there is, and thanks to Michael, we can share it here—it's Shift-Option-P (PC: Shift-Alt-P). Makes you want to buy Michael's book doesn't it? Now, for news of the weird: Although the Dodge, Burn, and Sponge tools enable you to use the Airbrush function, this cool undocumented keyboard shortcut won't work for those three tools. Another unsolved mystery.

   ## GIVE MOST ANYTHING A KEYBOARD SHORTCUT

Don't you wish there was a keyboard shortcut for Image Size? If you do (and I know you do), then make one. Go under the Edit menu and choose Keyboard Shortcuts. In the Shortcuts For pop-up menu choose Application Menus. In the window beneath the pop-up, double-click on the word Image to reveal all the menu commands in the Image menu. Scroll down and click on Image Size to

highlight its shortcut field, then press the keys for the shortcut you'd like to use, and click OK. That's it. And that's how you assign keyboard shortcuts for almost anything.

NO MORE UNLOCKING A BACKGROUND COPY

Back in Photoshop 7, if you made a copy of the Background layer (the fastest way is just to press Command-J [PC: Control-J]), the copy you made was locked (meaning you couldn't move it without unlocking it first). Well, Command-J (PC: Control-J) is still the fastest way to duplicate the Background layer, but in Photoshop CS, Adobe made things faster by automatically unlocking the Background layer for you. See, your Photoshop life is already getting better.

   SWAPPING CROP FIELDS

Adobe snuck a little button into the Options Bar that's hardly noticeable. It works with tools such as the Crop tool, and it's a big time saver. For example, for the Crop tool it swaps

the measurements in the Width and Height fields, so if you have the Crop tool set to crop to exactly a 5x7″, if you click this button (shown here), it will now crop to 7x5″. See? I told you it was handy.

LET THOSE WINDOWS BREATHE!

Since Photoshop 3.0, Photoshop has done something called "protecting the palettes" (I don't know if that's its official name, but we've always heard it called that). What it means is that as you increase the size of your image, Photoshop automatically stops increasing the size of the image window when it reaches the left edge of your open palettes. When it reaches this safety zone, the window stops growing, and only the image within the window continues to zoom. The only way to get around this (in previous versions of Photoshop) was to close your palettes. Then you could zoom the window as large as you'd like. However, Adobe addressed this problem back in Photoshop 6, and now if you want to keep the window growing, click on the Zoom tool, and up in the Options Bar, choose Ignore Palettes.

THE MULTIPLE UNDO SHORTCUT

Need to back up a few steps to readjust a setting? Piece of cake. Here's a shortcut to do just that. You can step back through your History palette by pressing Command-Option-Z (PC: Control-Alt-Z). This doesn't delete the items, but takes you back a step in the History palette.

WANT ARROWHEADS? PHOTOSHOP CAN ADD THEM FOR YOU!

This one is pretty slick because it's been a feature in Photoshop for a while, but eight out of ten Photoshop users will tell you Photoshop can't create arrowheads on the ends of lines (if it makes you feel any better, nine out of ten dentists didn't think Photoshop could do it either). Here's how: First, go under the Shape tools (in the Tool-box) and choose the Line tool. Then, up in the Options Bar, you'll see icons for the six shape tools. Directly to the right of these six icons is a down-facing triangle. Click on that triangle and out pops a dialog where you can click a

checkbox to add arrowheads to either the beginning or end of your line, and you can choose the Width, Length, and even the Concavity (there's that dentist thing again).

   GETTING TO THE FREE TRANSFORM TOOL'S POP-UP LIST

The Free Transform tool allows you to do all kinds of crazy stuff like Rotate, Skew, Flip Horizontal, and other cool stuff like that. The problem is, how can you remember all that stuff? Simple: Bring up Free Transform by pressing Command-T (PC: Control-T), then Control-click (PC: Right-click) inside the bounding box, and a pop-up menu will appear with a list of all the transformations you can choose from. You also get access to transformations, such as Flip Horizontal/Vertical, Rotate 180°, and Rotate 90° Clockwise/Counterclockwise, that don't have keyboard shortcuts at all.

DRAGGING AND DROPPING WHERE YOU WANT

If you drag an image from one document to another, the dragged image appears right at the spot where you let go of the mouse button. You may know that if you hold the Shift key when you drag-and-drop the image, the dragged image will automatically be centered within the receiving image. But you can go one better—make a selection in the receiving document, then hold the Shift key before you

drag. Your image will be centered within the selection, instead of within the entire document. Scary, isn't it? You can also copy-and-paste the selection and Photoshop will center the pasted image in the selection.

   CUSTOM BRUSHES DON'T HAVE TO BE SQUARE ANYMORE

In all previous versions of Photoshop, if you wanted to create your own custom brush, there was only one method—draw a square selection around the object that you wanted to become your custom brush, and then choose Define Brush under the Edit menu. In 7.0, Adobe took the chains off, and now not only can you use irregular selections to define a brush shape (like our baby brush here), you can also even use feathered selections. When the Brush Name dialog appears, name your brush and click OK. Your new brush will be added to the bottom of your Brushes palette.

FEATHER A SELECTION WITHOUT THE GUESSING GAME

Most of us try to guess how many pixels will give us the nice, soft selection we're looking for when we use the Feather Selection dialog. Sometimes we guess right, and other times we press Command-Z (PC: Control-Z) to undo the damage before trying again. Try this instead: Make your selection first, and then press "q" to turn on the Quick Mask mode. Now make the edge fade out by going under Filter, under Blur, and choosing Gaussian Blur. You can see how much of a blur you'll need to soften the edges as you adjust the Radius amount. When you're done, press "q" to get back to Standard mode with the selection already made with the exact amount of feathering that you want.

CREATING A FLATTENED VERSION OF YOUR LAYERED IMAGE

Alright, you're working on a Photoshop file that has a "bizillion" layers, and you want to create a new layer that's an exact copy of what your flattened image would look like. First, create a new blank layer by clicking on the New Layer icon at the bottom of the Layers palette, then hold Option (PC: Alt) and from the Layers palette's pop-down menu, choose Merge Visible. A flattened version of your image will appear on the new layer you created.

   IF IT'S NOT SQUARE, YOU CAN STILL CROP IT

Want to crop an image, but the area you want to keep is not a perfect square? Don't sweat it—just make a selection around the area you want to keep, using any selection tool you like (even the Lasso tool), and then choose Crop from the Image menu. It will crop the image as tightly as possible.

TOP-SECRET PHOTOSHOP SPLASH SCREEN

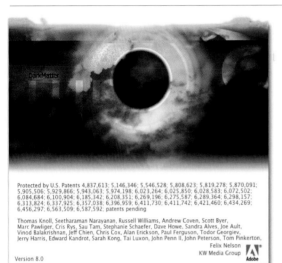

If you want to see the secret Photoshop beta startup screen (the pre-release version of Photoshop CS), just hold the Command key (PC: Control key) and choose "About Photoshop." It will show you the splash screen, displaying CS's secret pre-release code name. I'm telling you, those engineers know how to party.

 FALL IN LOVE WITH A TEMPORARY BRUSH, OR NOT

You can create a temporary brush anytime in Photoshop CS by playing with the options in the Brushes palette. After you make your choices, start painting. When you switch to another brush, the temporary brush you just created is gone. If you fall in love with your temporary brush (which is considered illegal in 48 states) and want to save it, before you change brush sizes, click on the Brush Sample up in the Options Bar, and when the Brush Picker appears, click on the New Preset Brush icon in the upper right-hand corner, you sick pup.

UNDO A SAVE? THAT'S IMPOSSIBLE, ISN'T IT?

This is a great trick we learned from our buddy Mike Ninness, and the first time we saw it, we said, "Hey, wait a minute, that can't be." Oh, but it be. It's how to undo a Save. This is especially helpful after you've flattened an image, saved the file, then realized that you needed to change something on a layer. This only happens to us about every other day, and here's the keyboard shortcut to fix it: Option-Command-Z (PC: Alt-Control-Z). Press it a few times after you've flattened and saved, and look in your Layers palette to see all the layers come a-rumbling right back. Pretty slick stuff.

   ## MAKE A PHOTOSHOP CLIENT PRESENTATION

To hide all your palettes and all your menus, and to display your current image centered on your monitor with a cool black frame around your image, just press the letter "f" twice, then press the Tab key (f, f, Tab). To return to your regular Photoshop work area, press "f," then Tab. You'll be the envy of all your friends, and eventually they'll write folk songs about you. It's almost embarrassing.

CHANGE BRUSH SOFTNESS ON THE FLY

You can increase or decrease the softness of a round brush in Photoshop without changing the size of the brush by pressing Shift-Left Bracket or Shift-Right Bracket. That's almost too easy.

LIGHTS, CAMERA, ACTION: SLIDE SHOWS USING PHOTOSHOP

You can create a mock slide show presentation by opening multiple images in Photoshop and then typing Control-Tab to rotate through the images. Plus, you can hold the Shift key and click on the Full Screen Mode icon near the bottom of your Toolbox to allow your images to fill the full screen (holding Shift will switch all of your open images to the Full Screen Mode at once). Finally, press Tab to hide your palettes and you're all set to give a slick presentation.

HOW TO CORRECT ONE PROBLEM COLOR

Let's say you have an image, but the sky doesn't look as vibrant as you'd like, and you want to increase the amount of blue without affecting the rest of the image. Try this on for size: Open an image that contains a daylight sky. Click on the New Adjustment Layer icon at the bottom of the Layers palette. In the pop-up menu, choose Color Balance. In the Color Balance dialog, drag the Blue all the way to the right (it looks bad now, but trust me), and click OK. Now, switch to the Brush tool. Press the letter "d" until your Foreground color is black, and with a large, soft brush, start painting over the areas you *don't* want blue. As you paint, the blue Color Balance you added is painted away. The sky is much bluer, but you can paint away the added blue from the other areas. To really see the before/after difference, click the Eye icon next to the Adjustment layer.

BUILDING A BETTER BACKGROUND ERASER TOOL

Here's a tip for making Photoshop's Background Eraser tool much more effective. Choose the Background Eraser tool, and in the Options Bar, lower the Tolerance setting to 20. In the Brushes palette, pick a large, hard-edged brush. Then, switch to the Pen tool, making sure that the paths icon (middle one at left in the Options Bar) is clicked. Draw a path just outside the edge of the object you want to isolate (you don't have to be precise; in fact, stay just outside the edges of the object and draw straight lines all the way around the image). Go to the Paths palette, and in the palette's pop-down menu, choose Stroke Path. When the dialog appears, under Tool, choose Background Eraser, and click OK. The Background Eraser will instantly trace around your image, following the path you created. Now that the edges have been erased, you can use the regular Eraser tool to erase the rest of the background area.

GETTING SIDE-BY-SIDE PREVIEWS

Want the ability to compare two photos at the same time? You can do it in the File Browser using this tip: First, click on the Expand button at the bottom center of the File Browser to hide the entire left column of palettes. This makes the thumbnail area take up the entire File Browser. Next, go under the File Browser's Edit menu and choose Preferences. Then set your Custom Thumbnail Size to around 400 pixels. Click OK, then go under View and choose Custom Thumbnail Size.

Now you've got huge thumbnails (as shown here). Just drag the bottom right-hand corner of the Browser out until you can see your two images side by side.

   CUSTOM BRUSHES: START WITH A CLEAN SLATE

If you're going to build your own custom brush in Photoshop CS, sometimes it's easier to start with an existing brush and edit it. The problem is that you may have all sorts of settings already in place (Texture, Scattering, Shape Dynamics, etc. along with all their individual options). To

set everything back to their defaults could take a while. At least it would if you didn't know this cool little trick: Click on the brush you want to use as your starting point for your custom brush, and in the Brushes palette, click on the options you want to edit (like Texture, Scattering, etc.). Then, from the palette's pop-down menu, choose Clear Brush Controls, and all the selected options will be instantly reset to their default settings.

TIMING IS EVERYTHING!

Want to know how long a particular Photoshop command takes? Click on the right-facing triangle toward the bottom left-hand corner of your image window. From the pop-up menu that appears, choose Timing. This starts the equivalent of a stopwatch that times your Photoshop commands in seconds. This is great for speed tests, pitting one machine against another. Which one runs the fastest Unsharp Mask? Time it and find out.

   INSTANT THUMBNAIL SIZE CONTROL

Want to change the size of your thumbnail preview in your Layers, Channels, or Paths palettes? Just hold the Control key (PC: Right-click) and click in an open area of the palette (such as the space under your Background layer, or beneath the bottom channel in the Channels palette), and a pop-up menu of thumbnail sizes will appear. You can choose from None, Small, Medium, or Large, instantly changing your thumbnail view.

BRING UP YOUR LAST PREFERENCE

Do you find yourself using Photoshop's Preferences quite often? If you do, you probably know there's a keyboard shortcut to bring up the General Preferences (Command-K/PC: Control-K), but there's actually a cooler tip—how to bring up the last Preference dialog you were in. Since Photoshop has eight different Preference dialogs, it can save you some significant time digging through the submenus. To bring up the last Preference dialog you used, press Option-Command-K (PC: Alt-Control-K).

Burn Rubber

TYPE

TIPS

Do you remember the song "Burn Rubber" by the Gap Band from back in the early 80s? Remember it goes: "Burn rubber on me, Charlene…

Burn Rubber

smokin' type tips

whoa, no…." Not ringing any bells? It doesn't matter. This chapter has nothing to do with burning rubber—I was just curious to see if you're as old as I am (which is young. Very young. I heard that song accidentally on an oldies station in my dad's car).

This chapter is dedicated to making the time you spend using type in Photoshop more productive. Here's the weird thing about Photoshop type—back in version 6, Adobe added most of the high-end typography features found in Adobe's high-end page layout program, InDesign. Which made me think, "Why?" I can't imagine setting a book or magazine article in Photoshop, because when Photoshop type gets below 12 points, it starts to get fuzzy, so laying out columns of text and tweaking the balance, spacing, and paragraph specs for columns of type just doesn't make sense. Then I figured out what's going on. Somebody at Adobe must be hittin' the crack pipe. Could that be it? Or is it so not, that it freaks you out.

GETTING TYPE IN A PERFECT CIRCLE

Now that Photoshop CS can really give you type in a circle, getting a perfect circle that you can add type to is not as obvious as you'd think. To get this perfect circle, click on the Shape tools in the Toolbox and choose the Ellipse tool from the flyout menu. Then go up to the Options Bar, and in the second group of icons from the left, click on the middle icon, which creates a regular path, rather than a Shape layer or a pixel-based shape. Then, hold the Shift key, and drag out your circle (the Shift key constrains the shape to a perfect circle). Now you can move your Type tool over the circle, and it will change into a Type on a Path cursor. Click on the circle, and get to typin'.

I NEED MY DUMB QUOTES AGAIN

In all previous versions of Photoshop, when you typed in a quotation mark (") or apostrophe ('), what Photoshop gave you was the straight-up-and-down inch mark (") or foot mark (') instead. They're called "dumb quotes." Luckily, back in Photoshop 7.0, Adobe brought these typographically challenged dummies into line, and now they're properly applied as "curly quotes" by default, which is great. That is unless you have to actually type an inch mark or a foot mark. Here's the workaround—when it comes time to type in an inch or foot mark, go under the Photoshop menu, under Preferences, and choose General (in Windows, Preferences can be found under the Edit menu). In the General Preferences dialog, turn off Use Smart Quotes, and then type in your characters. When you're done, return to the General Preferences and turn them back on to bring typographic order to your world.

RESETTING YOUR TYPE

If you're into typography, Photoshop CS gives you loads of typographical control. You can adjust everything from tracking, kerning, and dozens of other characteristics. The downside is—the Character palette (where we make most of these tweaks) keeps your last used settings as a default. If you did some major type tweaking to your last line of type, it might need some major "un-doing" in the Character palette to get you back to normal type settings. Rather than manually resetting every field, to quickly reset Photoshop's type to its "default" standard settings, just go to the Character palette, and choose Reset Character from the palette's pop-down menu.

● ◐ ◐ **ONE-CLICK ACCESS TO THE COPYRIGHT SYMBOL, AND MORE**

Looking for some special type characters, like ©, ™, or ®? If you're not fussy about these characters actually being a font, you can find them in the default set of Custom Shapes. Just get the Custom Shape tool, click on the Shape Picker up in the Options Bar, and you'll find all three special characters there, in the default set of shapes.

HIGHLIGHTING YOUR TEXT SUPER FAST!

When you want to automatically highlight the type from a Type layer and switch to the Type tool at the same time to make some copy changes, just double-click directly on the "T" icon in the Layers palette, next to the Type layer you want to edit, and blam! You're ready to go.

   RENDERING TEXT IN JUST ONE CLICK

If you need to convert your Type layer into an image layer, you can save some time by simply holding the Control key (PC: Right-click) and clicking directly on the Type layer name that appears in the Layers palette. A pop-up menu will appear where you can choose Rasterize Layer to instantly render your type.

MADE TO FIT

To create a "text box" for your type to fit within, select the Type tool, then click-and-drag out the area you want for your text box. Your type will now fit within that box. When you're finished entering your text, just press Enter to get out of the text bounding box.

   TEXT-PATH-MAKING MANIAC

If you want to convert your Type layer into paths (so it looks as if you meticulously drew the type with the Pen tool—your clients won't have to know), simply go under the Layer menu, under Type, and choose Create Work Path.

PICTURE THIS: PUTTING A PHOTO INSIDE TYPE

First, set your Foreground color to black (by pressing "d"). Choose the Type tool and create your text (you don't have to rasterize the type). Then, open the image you want to appear inside your type and use the Move tool to drag it into your type document. (It should appear on the layer above your Type layer. If it doesn't, just go to the Layers palette and move it on top of your Type layer.) To put your image inside the type, press Command-G (PC: Control-G) and whammo—your image is masked into your type. You can reposition the image by using the Move tool. And since you didn't rasterize your Type layer, your text remains totally editable—just click on the Type layer and start editing. You can add Layer Styles to your Type layer to further enhance the effect. If you're not crazy about the image you picked, press Shift-Command-G (PC: Shift-Control-G) and remove the image.

FONTS, FONTS, AND MORE FONTS

Here's a tip to quickly change typefaces and see the change while you make it. First, highlight the type you want to change, and then press Command-H (PC: Control-H) to hide the highlighting (the type is still highlighted; the highlight is just hidden from view). Then, up in the Options Bar, click once in the font field, then use the Up/Down Arrow keys on your keyboard to scroll through your installed typefaces. Man, do I love this one.

 MAKE YOUR TEXT JUMP INTO ACTION

Earlier, I gave you the quick tip for rasterizing your type by Control-clicking (PC: Right-clicking) on your Type layer in the Layers palette, then choosing Rasterize Layer from the pop-up menu that appears. Believe it or not, there's an even faster way, if you don't mind spending a minute or two up front setting it up, by creating an Action that rasterizes the type for you with just one key. Here's how: Create a Type layer, then make the Actions palette visible. Choose New Action from the Actions palette pull-down menu (the circle with the right-facing arrow in it). Name your new Action "Rasterize Type Layers," then, from the F-key pop-up menu, assign an F-key to this Action. Click the Record button (it's where the OK button usually is), then go under the Layer menu, under Rasterize, and choose Type. Now go

back to the Actions palette and click on the Stop button at the bottom of the palette (it's the first button from the left). That's it—your Action is written. Test it by creating a Type layer, then pressing the F-key you assigned to your Action. It should instantly rasterize (you'll know if it worked, because the "T" icon on the Type layer will no longer be visible).

DOUBLE YOUR PLEASURE

We've already talked about rasterizing text, but once you've rasterized your Type layer into a regular image layer, your type is no longer editable (meaning you can't go back and change type faces, type in a different word, adjust leading or kerning, etc.). Here's a quick way around that limitation. Before rasterizing (rendering) your type, duplicate the Type layer by dragging it to the New Layer icon at the bottom of the Layers palette. Then, hide the original Type layer from view (by clicking on the Eye icon next to the original Type layer). That way, if you ever need to go back and change the word (or font, leading, etc.), you have the original editable Type layer still available. Just simply make it visible.

   SEEING YOUR TYPE CHANGE COLOR

In Photoshop, you can change the color of your type without even selecting it first. "Why is that important?" you may ask. If you highlight your type to change its color using the Foreground Color Swatch in the Toolbox, the highlighting hides the color of your type so you can't see any of your color changes while you're in the Color Picker. So instead, after you commit your type by pressing the Enter key, click on the Color Swatch in the Options Bar (without highlighting your type first). As you change colors in the Color Picker, you'll see your type update on the fly.

MOVE YOUR TYPE, WITHOUT SWITCHING TOOLS

Here's a tip that can save you a lot of tool switching when formatting your type. Once you create your type and while your cursor is still blinking somewhere in the text, if you need to move the type, you don't have to switch to the Move tool—just move your Type cursor away from your type (either above, below, or an inch or so to the right or left), and your cursor will temporarily change to the Move tool. You can now simply click-and-drag your type. If you want to edit your type some more, just move your cursor back to the type and click where you need to make edits.

   ## EDITING TEXT WITHOUT HIGHLIGHTING IT

Here's a cool little tip for changing your font size without having the Type tool active. Just click on your Type layer (in the Layers palette), then go under the Window menu and choose Character. When the Character palette appears, you can make changes to your type size, color, font, tracking, etc. It freaks you out, doesn't it?

RASTERIZE TIMES 2, 4, 6...

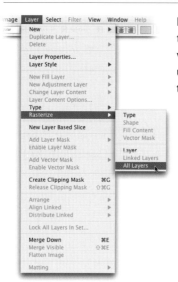

If you have multiple Type layers and you want to convert them all to image layers, there's a way to do it without individually rasterizing each. Simply go under the Layer menu, under Rasterize, and choose All Layers. This will rasterize all the Type layers at once.

   HONEY, I NEED SOME SPACE: VISUALLY ADJUST KERNING

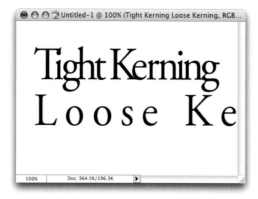

You can visually control the spacing between your type (which is much better than numerically trying to figure it out) by using the same keyboard shortcuts for adjusting type that Adobe Illustrator uses. Here's how: To set the tracking tighter (tightening the space between each letter or word in a group), highlight the type then press Option-Left Arrow (PC: Alt-Left Arrow) to tighten. Press Option-Right Arrow (PC: Alt-Right Arrow) to add more space between a selected group of letters or words. To adjust the space between two individual letters (called kerning) click your cursor between the two letters and use the same keyboard shortcuts mentioned above.

TELL PHOTOSHOP WHEN YOU'RE DONE WITH TYPE

As you probably know, you can jump to most any tool in the Toolbox by pressing a single-key keyboard shortcut. (If you didn't know that, sell your copy of Photoshop. Kidding. Just turn to Chapter 2 for some essential tips.) Here's the problem: While creating type with the Type tool, if you press one of those one-key shortcuts (let's say the letter "p" for the Pen tool), instead of jumping to the Pen tool, Photoshop types the letter "p". It'll drive you nuts. Okay, you won't go nuts, but at the very least you'll have a lot of typos. The reason is this: You have to tell Photoshop that you're done editing your type. You do this in one of three ways: (1) Click on the check icon at the far right of the Options Bar, (2) press the Enter key, or (3) switch to another tool manually by clicking on it in the Toolbox. Any of these three options tells Photoshop that you're done and lets you use the single-key shortcuts to switch tools.

   BRING THOSE TYPE LAYERS TOGETHER

How do you merge two Type layers together? Unfortunately, while they're still editable Type layers, you can't—you have to rasterize the layers first. Technically, you rasterize just one (the bottom of the two Type layers), and then make the top Type layer active and press Command-E (PC: Control-E) to merge these two layers together. However, when you do that, the top Type layer will automatically rasterize as the two layers are combined into one, so there's really no way around it—with the exception of this little tip: Highlight the editable type on the top layer and choose Cut from the Edit menu. Switch to the lower Type layer, click your Type cursor once at the end of the type, press Return (PC: Enter) to start a new line, then choose Paste from the Edit menu to paste the contents of the top Type layer into the bottom Type layer. Then drag the old top Type layer into the Trash icon at the bottom of the Layers palette. Although it takes a little effort, now you have both layers combined into one layer (your goal), but the type remains totally editable (the bonus).

THE LONG AND THE SHORT OF TYPE

Although the Character palette has numeric controls for making your type fatter (horizontal scaling) or taller (vertical scaling), it's usually easier to do these two functions visually (rather than numerically). Here's how: First set your type, then with the type cursor still blinking somewhere in the text, press-and-hold the Command key (PC: Control key) to bring up the Free Transform bounding box. To make your type fatter, click on the center handle on either side, release the Command key (PC: Control key), and drag outward. To make your type taller, grab the center handle on the top or bottom, release the Command key (PC: Control key), and drag upward or downward.

MADE TO FIT: PART TWO

This tip relates to a previous tip, where you created what's called a "text box" so that your type wraps within a text block, rather than running in one straight line. The tip is this: If you've created some standard type by just clicking and typing rather than creating a paragraph text block, you're not out of luck. While the Type layer is active, just go under the Layer menu, under Type, and choose Convert to Paragraph Text. Now your type will wrap within text box boundaries, and you can edit the boundaries by adjusting the corner and center points.

MAKING THE SPELL CHECKER OBEY YOUR COMMANDS

Photoshop's spell checker isn't just window dressing; it has a very robust spell-checking function, akin to Adobe InDesign's own spell checker, but if you understand how it works, you can save yourself some time and frustration. Basically, if you highlight some text on a layer, it checks just the highlighted text, so if you highlight one word, it just checks that one word (even if there are dozens of words in your paragraph). If you choose to spell check but don't have anything highlighted, it checks your entire document, regardless of how many Type layers you have. It's also helpful to know that it only checks real Type layers (layers that have a capital "T" as their thumbnail image in the Layers palette), and it cannot spell-check any layers with text that have been rasterized (converted from a Type layer into a regular image layer).

   EDITING TYPE ON A PATH

If you've created some type on a path, highlighting that type to edit it (to change the font, color, spelling, etc.) can be kind of tricky. That's why it's quicker to go to the Layers palette and double-click directly on the "T" thumbnail icon. This will highlight all the type on this layer, making it easy to type in some new text, or change some of the attributes.

EXACT SIZING FOR YOUR TEXT COLUMNS

We already showed you how to create a column of type by clicking-and-dragging the Type tool to create your "text box" so your text will wrap within that column. But here's a quick little tip that lets you tell Photoshop exactly the width and height you'd like your type column to be (rather than just clicking-and dragging it out visually). With the Type tool, just hold the Option key (PC: Alt key) and click in your document and the Paragraph Text Size dialog will appear where you can enter the exact size you'd like for your column.

   REMOVING THOSE TYPOGRAPHICALLY INCORRECT SPACES

If you're trying to set type that looks typographically correct in Photoshop, there's an old habit you'll have to break, and that's the curse of putting two spaces at the end of every sentence. This is a holdover from people who at one time used traditional typewriters, where adding two spaces was necessary, but in typesetting that's a huge no-no. About 70% of the text I copy and paste from text files that people give me has two spaces, but I use this Photoshop tip to fix the problem in just seconds. First, go under the Edit menu and choose Find and Replace Text. In the Find field, press the Spacebar twice (entering two spaces), then in Change To, press the Spacebar just once. Click Change All, and every time Photoshop finds two spaces at the end of a sentence, it will replace it with just one, making you typographically correct.

TWEAK ALL YOUR TYPE IN ONE FELL SWOOP!

This is a pretty darn slick tip for changing the font, size, or color of a number of different Type layers all at once. Here's how it's done: First, link all the layers that you want to adjust by clicking in the second column beside each Type layer. Once all the layers are linked, hold the Shift key and make your change. The change you make to one Type layer will also affect all the linked Type layers. The key is *not to* highlight your type. Just choose the Type tool and go straight to the Options Bar or the Character palette. Schweeeet!

DON'T HAVE ITALIC OR BOLD? DON'T SWEAT IT

If you have a typeface that doesn't have a bold or italic version available, don't sweat it—Photoshop can make a fake bold or italic version for you. They're called faux bold and faux italic (don't pronounce them "fox bold" or the French will get really cranky about it. It's pronounced "fo," as in "Fe, Fi, Fo, Fum"). To apply a faux style to the type, highlight your type and choose Faux Bold or Faux Italic from the Character palette's pop-down menu. Here's another tip: Don't forget to turn off these faux styles when you're done, because they don't automatically turn themselves off. Vive le Français!

The reason I call this chapter "Killer Web Tips" is because most of the tips in this chapter came from a buddy of mine who's now serving time in Rayford

Fast & Furious

killer web tips

State Penitentiary for manslaughter. Technically, he's not really a killer, and technically this chapter should have been called "Web Tips From a Killer" rather than "Killer Web Tips," but really, would you have bought this book if that was the name of this chapter? You would have? Wow! You're my kind of person (or trustee, as my friend likes to call them).

Seriously though, in this chapter we're going to look at some tips to make optimizing your graphics easier and faster, while making your file sizes as small as possible. If you incorporate these tips into your Web work, before you know it, you'll be earning more money, and then when you have enough money, you can buy cartons of cigarettes to bribe the guards. See, it all works out in the end.

LOSE THOSE ANNOYING NUMBERS IN THE UPPER LEFT-HAND CORNER

We get more letters from people who ask us, "How do I get rid of that number in the top left-hand corner of my image?" This little puppy appears if you accidentally click on the Slice tool in the Toolbox. Even if you notice your error and immediately switch to another tool, it's too late. The "slice number" is already in place. To make it go away, go under the View menu, under Show, and choose Slices. Then try not to accidentally click on the Slice tool again. (Sorry, I just felt like scolding somebody, you know, just for fun.)

NEED TO SHRINK THE FILE SIZE? USE TRANSPARENCY

Want a killer tip for squeezing even more size out of your GIF Web images? Make something transparent. That's right, if you can pick an area of your image to make transparent, your file size will drop like a rock. For example, if you're putting a logo over a white background and you can make the white area around the logo transparent, your file size will be significantly smaller. The transparent areas are virtually ignored when determining file size, because, after all, there's nothing there.

CROP IT EVEN CLOSER

When you're designing graphics for the Web, you don't want even one extra pixel of unused space, because it adds to the overall file size of the image. Because of that, you want to crop your Web graphics as tightly as possible. Luckily for us (you, them, etc.), Photoshop CS can do it for you automatically. Just choose Trim from the Image menu, click OK in the dialog, and it will crop your Web graphic as tightly as possible for the smallest possible file size. It does this by looking at the pixel color in the upper left-hand corner of your image and cropping down until it hits another color. (Note: The Trim dialog also gives you the option to base the crop on the bottom right-hand corner pixel color or transparent areas). This works especially well when creating type for the Web, because you'll often create it on a white background.

 LET PHOTOSHOP MAKE THE FILE SIZE CALL

Oftentimes you have a target size you're trying to hit when creating Web graphics; for example, you're creating a Web banner and your file size limit is 32 K. If that's the case, and you know the target size, why not let Photoshop do all the work? Here's how: Under the File menu, go to Save for Web. In the Save for Web dialog, just to the right of the Settings pop-up menu, is a right-facing triangle. Click-and-hold it and when the pop-up menu appears, choose Optimize to File Size. In the dialog, enter the target file size you need your graphic to be and click OK to have Photoshop optimize the graphic to fit your target file size. If it doesn't matter to you whether it's a GIF or JPEG, choose Auto Select GIF/JPEG and Photoshop will make the call.

ZOOM OUT FOR SHARPER WEB IMAGES

This is a tip we use almost daily when we have to greatly reduce the size and/or resolution of an image. Sometimes when you make a drastic size/resolution change, it can really make the resulting image blurry, so what we do is simply zoom out on the image so that the window and image are at either 50% or 25% view. Then, we take a screen capture of our image window at the new smaller size. That way, the image still looks sharp, but it's much smaller when we open the screen capture in Photoshop. The trick to making this work is using either a 50%, 25%, or 12.5% view size for making the capture. If you view the image at 66.7%, 33.3%, or 16.7%, the image won't be as crisp (because of the way Photoshop draws the image at those views).

   IMAGEREADY FEATURE COMES TO PHOTOSHOP

One of our favorite little features from Adobe ImageReady has made its way into Photoshop—it's called Slices From Guides. What it does is slice your image (for the Web) where your guides are positioned. To make use of this handy little number, just make your rulers visible, drag out guides where you'd like your slices applied, and then switch to the Slice tool (press the letter "k"). Once you've got the Slice tool, look up in the Options Bar and you'll find a button called Slices From Guides. Click the button and Photoshop will do the rest.

TWO EASY WAYS TO CREATE TRANSPARENCY

The most common method for making a background tranparent back in Photoshop 6.0 is still available to you in Photoshop CS, and that's to go to the Layers palette and simply delete the Background layer. That's it. This leaves only the layers that were above the Background layer (which already have background transparency). Now, there's another easy way, and that's to go to Photoshop's Save for Web command, switch to the Eyedropper tool in the Save for Web's Toolbox, and click on the background color you want to become transparent. Then, just below the Color Table on the bottom right of the dialog, click on the first icon, which creates transparency from your selected color.

   IMAGEREADY WINDOW SPEED TIP

If you're using Adobe ImageReady (which comes installed with Photoshop as part of the package), by default the image window displays the original (unoptimized version) of your image. However, if you want to quickly view the optimized version, a 2-Up version (original and optimized side by side), or the 4-Up version (your original and three other optimized options), you can use the quick tip Command-Y (PC: Control-Y) to rotate through your four view choices. A big time saver.

IF IT'S WEB SAFE, DON'T USE IT

The one Color palette that we absolutely don't use at all anymore is the Web-safe Color palette. Why? You don't need it—and it can make your file sizes significantly larger than necessary. The Web-safe colors were created back when most computer users had computers that could only display a maximum of 256 colors. Out of those 256, the "Web-safe" colors were the 216 colors that were the same on both Macintosh and Windows browsers. Even back then you could still use a non-Web-safe color, but it might dither to the next closest Web-safe color so the color might be off a bit. Luckily these days, you'd be hard-pressed to find anyone using such a lame computer that it only displays 256 colors. They haven't sold a computer like that for literally years. If you've ever looked at a row of monitors at the computer store, you'll notice the color is slightly different on every one, but that's another story.

   CHANGE ONE PREFERENCE, SAVE A BUNDLE

If you're creating Web graphics with Photoshop and you're *not* using the Save for Web feature (which is perfectly fine not to do), make sure you go under the Photoshop menu (in Mac OS X), under Preferences, and choose File Handling (in Windows, Preferences can be found under the Edit menu). In the Image Previews pop-up, change the setting from Always Save to Never Save. Image Previews are those tiny thumbnail icons that are visible on your system. They look cute, but they take up big space—often accounting for 70% of your file size. Turn them off, and you'll save file size big time. (Save for Web does this automatically, so if you're using that feature, don't sweat it.)

GET THE REAL 100% VIEW

When creating Web graphics, it's often important to view your graphic at the same size your audience will view it. To view your image at 100%, just double-click on the Zoom tool. If your image is too big when viewed at 100%, just zoom out until the view of your image is the size you'd like it to appear on the Web page (use the zoom-out shortcuts—Zoom tool holding the Option/Alt keys, etc.), then look in the lower left corner of the image window and you'll see the percentage of zoom. Write that down, then go under the Image menu and choose Image Size. When the Image Size dialog appears, in the Height pop-up menu in the Pixel Dimensions section, choose Percent. Then enter the percentage amount you wrote down earlier. By default, Photoshop will enter the Width when you enter the Height setting to keep your image proportional (make sure the Constrain Proportions checkbox is turned on at the bottom). Click OK and it resizes your image to the exact size you want it to appear on the Web page.

   STYLE WARNING FOR WEB DESIGNERS

If you're designing Web graphics using Photoshop and ImageReady, you're probably spending a decent amount of time swapping back and forth between the two apps. Although the two programs share many of the same features and commands, one thing they don't share is custom Styles that you've saved in Photoshop's Styles palette. So just be forewarned: If you create a custom style in Photoshop, don't expect to find that same style in ImageReady.

SPEND MORE TIME ANIMATING, LESS TIME CLICKING

If you're building Web animations in ImageReady, you don't have to keep clicking the tiny controls at the bottom of the Animations palette. Instead, navigate using these quick shortcuts: To play your animation, press Shift-Spacebar. To stop it, press Shift-Spacebar again. Press Option-Left Arrow (PC: Alt-Left Arrow) to go to the previous frame. Press Option-Right Arrow (PC: Alt-Right Arrow) to go to the next frame. To quickly jump back to the beginning of your animation, press Shift-Option-Left Arrow (PC: Shift-Alt-Left Arrow).

GETTING TO THE HEXADECIMAL CODE

As you may know, there are hexadecimal codes for the colors used in Web pages. Not only does Photoshop know these hexadecimal codes, it can extract them from an image and let you paste them into your HTML code editor. First, press the letter "i" to switch to the Eyedropper tool, and then hold the Control key (PC: Right-click) and click on a color within your image. A pop-up menu will appear where you can choose Copy Color as HTML. Now you can switch to your HTML editor and choose Paste to copy the HTML code into your app.

GET SUPER-CLEAN TYPE FOR THE WEB

If you've been faced with having to create small type on the Web (usually 12 points or below), you know the smaller you go, the blurrier your type gets. That's because of the anti-aliasing that's automatically applied to the type, which works fine at larger sizes but tends to run together at smaller sizes, making your type look fuzzy. You can adjust the amount of aliasing (from the Options Bar), but here's a tip that many Web designers feel works even better: Once you get below 12 points, start adding positive tracking to your type (anywhere between 20 to 50 points) in the Character palette. This increases the amount of space between letters and, therefore, decreases the amount of blurriness.

Increasing the space between your letters this way minimizes the effects of anti-aliasing and makes your type cleaner and more readable at smaller sizes. As a general rule—the smaller the type, the larger the tracking amount.

GOT A FOLDER FULL OF IMAGES FOR THE WEB? BATCH 'EM!

Do you have a whole folder of images that you're going to convert to Web graphics? If the images are somewhat similar, don't do them one at a time—automate the process using Actions. Start by opening one image from the folder. Go to the Actions palette and click on the New Action button. Give this action a name (something like Optimize as JPEGs) then go about the business of optimizing this one graphic into a JPEG for the Web. When you're done optimizing it, click the Stop button at the bottom of the Actions palette. Then go under the File menu, under Automate, and choose Batch. In this dialog, under Play, choose the name of the new action you just created. Under Source, choose the folder of images you want converted using that action, and under Destination, choose what you want to happen to those images after they're converted. Click OK, and Photoshop will convert that folder with absolutely blinding speed. This one tip can really change the way you work, especially if you create for print first, then repurpose for the Web.

EXERCISING YOUR INFLUENCE ON GIFS

This is an old trick we use to influence how Photoshop builds its color table when creating GIF images. We put a selection around the area of the image that's most important to us (for example, if we had a product shot, we'd put a selection around it), then we'd convert to Index Color. Photoshop will look at the colors contained in your selection and build the Indexed Color Table giving preference to those colors. It's another slick way to use fewer colors, creating a smaller file but with a better-looking image.

   READ THE WEB COLOR ONSCREEN

Want to know the hexadecimal Web color values of any color in your image? The Info palette can tell you instantly. Go under the Window menu and choose Show Info. In the Info palette, click on the little Eyedropper icon next to the CMYK readout and a pop-up menu appears. Choose Web Color, and you'll get the hexadecimal readouts right in the palette.

IMAGEREADY'S SUPERCHARGED EYEDROPPER

In previous versions of Photoshop, you could only use the Eyedropper tool to sample a color from other open images in Photoshop, but for some reason ImageReady had a supercharged Eyedropper. If you held the mouse button down, you could leave your image window and sample colors from, well, just about anything—including your computer desktop or any other open application. Freaky! Fortunately, Adobe finally added this same power to Photoshop 7.0's Eyedropper tool.

IMAGEREADY'S AUTO TILE MAKER

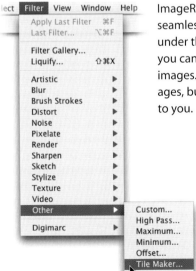

ImageReady has a built-in seamless tile creator for creating seamless backgrounds. It's called Tile Maker and it's found under the Filter menu, under Other. It brings up a dialog where you can choose how much you want to blend the edges of your images. The default setting of 10 works fairly well for most images, but you can increase it if it doesn't look smooth enough to you.

MAKE SURE YOU SEE IT THE SAME WAY THEY SEE IT

If you're designing Web graphics on a Macintosh, you can be sure they're going to be viewed by lots of people using a PC, and vice versa. A design problem arises because the monitors on Macs and on PCs display with different levels of brightness. For example, if you design Web graphics on a Macintosh, they'll look more than 10% darker when viewed on a PC using Windows. Photoshop will let you see an approximation of how those graphics will look when viewed on a PC. Here's how: Choose Save for Web from the File menu. Then, at the top right of the preview window you'll see a pop-up menu called the Preview Menu. From that menu, choose Standard Windows Color to get a preview of how your currently opened graphic will look when viewed on a standard Windows monitor. Windows designers can do the same thing and view how their Web graphics will look when viewed on a Mac (they'll look lighter). Knowing how your graphics will look on each platform will help you find a happy middle ground that looks good on both.

   DON'T LOAD THAT BOGUS SLICE!

If you're slicing images for the Web in Photoshop (using the Slice tool), here's a tip to save even more space. If you have a slice in your image that's going to be the same color as your background (for example, you've got a solid white slice going on a solid white background), you can save file size by having that slice load no image at all. Sound like a plan? (I thought you'd like that.) Here's how to do it: Once your slice is in place, make it active (using the Slice Select tool), and then click on the Slice Options button in the Options Bar. A dialog will appear, and in the Slice Type pop-up menu, choose No Image and click OK. That way, when Photoshop generates its HTML for the page, there will be no image in that spot, just the white background showing through, giving you a faster loading Web page. Pretty sweet!

USE LAYER-BASED SLICES

If you're getting ready to slice an image for the Web and you still have your layers intact, don't flatten that image before you slice. Instead, let Photoshop create the (layer-based) slices for you. There are two main advantages: (1) it's easier. You don't have to drag out slices—Photoshop does it automatically, perfectly slicing at the size of your layer. But even better is (2), when you create a layer-based slice, you can move the layer, and (get this) Photoshop will automatically adjust all the slices to accommodate your move, and it will create a new slice for your layer as well. If you slice manually and move your layer—you're out of luck—the old slice stays right where it was. Plus, creating a layer-based slice couldn't be easier. Click on the layer you want to slice, then go under the Layer menu and choose New Layer Based Slice—Photoshop does the rest.

   ## BLUR THAT JPEG AND SHRINK IT DOWN

Here's a cool tip for when you're creating JPEG images. This tip doesn't work for all images but can really come in handy for others. The tip is this: Because of the way JPEG compression works, if you can slightly blur your image, the file size will be smaller. You could just add a Gaussian Blur, or you could blur the image directly from the Save for Web dialog by entering a number in the Blur field. However, you're usually better off putting a selection around the important areas of your image, then inverting the selection and blurring just the background. That way, the important parts stay sharp, and the noncritical areas become more compressed.

Fast Company

DESIGN TIPS

As I'm sure you've noticed by now, this book is filled with Photoshop topic-specific tips, such as layers tips or production tips, but there's a whole

Fast Company

photoshop design tips

subset of tips that aren't as much about pressing a keyboard shortcut or a hidden command as they are about what we've learned while working in our studio on real-world projects.

Unfortunately, the studio we work in is a hair studio, so many of our tips are like, "Use Paul Mitchell products" or "Lather, rinse, and repeat," so I'm not sure how helpful they'll be, but I guarantee you this—you'll have shiny, more manageable hair in just two weeks.

Okay, they're actually Photoshop tips, but they answer questions that are much broader, such as "How far is the drop shadow supposed to be from an object?", "How do I scan a three-dimensional object?", or "How much conditioner should I use for a dry, oily scalp?" Did you catch that "dry oily" oxymoron? You didn't? I'm not sure you're ready for these tips. Apply a cream rinse, then we'll talk.

EFFECTIVE GHOSTING OR BACKSCREENING

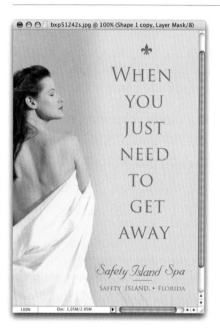

Ghosting, or backscreening, a photographic image is another very effective design technique. This is a fantastic way to isolate text, logos, or other graphic elements in a photographic image. Simply choose the areas you wish to ghost, or screen (using the selection tool of your choice). Bring up the Levels dialog, and move the midtone Input Levels slider (the one in the center) toward the left. Note: When placing text over a ghosted area, be sure to lighten it enough so that your text will be legible.

  ## TWO-COLOR MAY BE BETTER THAN FOUR

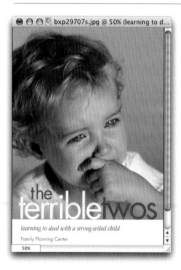

Sometimes we get so obsessed with the four-color process that we forget that we can oftentimes convey the same visual message with two colors. Photoshop gives us amazing control over duotones. Combine that with good use of tints and screens and we can achieve some amazing effects. Not only that, but your clients will fall head over heels for you when they realize that you just saved them some fat dinero.

OVERLAP GRAPHIC ELEMENTS TO ADD VISUAL INTEREST

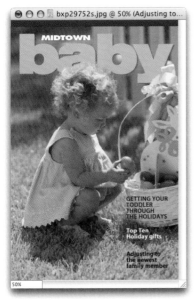

A great way to add visual interest to any design project is to overlap an image over text. This simple technique will add depth to your design project, giving even a simple newsletter or masthead a more dramatic visual impact.

First, place your text or nameplate over a background image. Now, go back to the background image in the Layers palette and select the areas you want to overlap the text (using the selection tool of your choice). Place this selection on its own layer by pressing Command-J (PC: Control-J), then move it to the top of the Layers palette above your text or nameplate layer. It's that simple.

FOCUSING ATTENTION BY ADDING DEPTH

Here's a trick for defining depth to the viewer of your artwork: Make the objects that are farther away appear out of focus or blurry, and the objects that are near, sharp and crisp. You can use this technique for drawing attention to objects in the foreground of your Photoshop image by slightly blurring the background. This adds depth and dimension to your artwork, as well as focusing attention. To do this, put a selection around the area you want the focus, add a 10-pixel Feather (Option-Command-D/Alt-Control-D), Inverse the selection (from the Select menu or Shift-Command-I/Shift-Control-I), then apply your Blur (Filter>Blur>Gaussian).

FOCUSING ATTENTION USING COLOR

You've seen this effect done over and over again in commercials. Here's a quick technique to focus attention using color. Open an image. Press Shift-Command-U (PC: Shift-Control-U) to Desaturate the image. Choose the History Brush from the Toolbox. Open the History palette and click on the column to the left of the History State that says "Open." Now simply paint back in the areas you wish to remain full color.

   DON'T MAKE IT BLACK—MAKE IT MEGA BLACK!

If you're creating a black background for something that will appear in print, don't just fill the background with 100% black. For that rich-looking, deep black, you need to have a custom black build (we call it mega black) for that "midnight black" effect when printed. Our favorite black build is C=75, M=50, Y=50, and K=100. Most traditional print houses use what they call a cyan kicker in their blacks, which is a black color build using 75% cyan and 100% black, but we feel our mega black build is much, well, blacker! Give it a try and see if you agree.

SHADOW OPACITY AND SOFTNESS

The softness (or blurriness) and the opacity (or transparency) of a shadow depends on how close the object casting the shadow is to the background or object that it's casting the shadow onto. The rule to follow is this: The farther away the object, the softer and less opaque the shadow will be (see example on left). Take a look at the settings we used in the Layer Style/Drop Shadow dialog. The Opacity was lowered to 30% to make it more transparent. The Distance is 35 pixels so that the floating type looks farther away from the background, and the Size (softness or blur) is set to 15 pixels to give it a soft (blurry) edge. Together, this gives the text the appearance of being higher, or farther away from the background.

Now the closer the object, the shadow will have harder edges and be more opaque (see example on left). Once again, look at the settings we used to create our shadow. This time we made the shadow more opaque by raising the Opacity to 40%, and we lowered both the Distance and the Size. Without ever moving our text, we made our type look closer to the background just by changing the softness and opacity of the drop shadow.

CREATE YOUR OWN CUSTOM TYPEFACE

Photoshop's Type tool gives us the flexibility to customize our fonts by converting the font to paths or selections. In the past, we'd have to customize the fonts in other vector-based applications and then import them into our Photoshop file. Forget that; here's a better way: Open a new Photoshop file and type in some text using the Type tool. Go under Layer, under Type, and choose Convert to Shape. Now, use the Direct Selection tool to select individual points, and move them wherever you want (as you move the points, your layer shape automatically fills in). It's that easy.

  USE CORRECT CMYK BUILDS TO MATCH PANTONE COLORS

You're working on a Photoshop project, and you want to match a specific Pantone color build. Find the CMYK formula (for the specific Pantone color) from a current Pantone color formula guide, and use that to build your color in Photoshop. Photoshop's CMYK color simulation may not match the printed color standard.

ADD COLOR TO YOUR SHADOWS

Adding color to a shadow is a quick way to give any layout a nice design twist. Matching the shadow to a surrounding color or other graphic element is a great way to tie the layout together. Click on the Add a Layer Style icon (the black circle with the little "*f*" in it) and choose Drop Shadow. Click on the Color Swatch and select a color from your image by moving your cursor over the image (your cursor will turn into an Eyedropper) and clicking on the color. You can edit the shadow settings to achieve the desired results. If you want to put another artsy twist on it (and we do), make a custom shadow with the Gradient tool and use Free Transform to add some perspective.

PICKING COLORS? USE THE BUILT-IN COLOR WHEEL

If you need some help in picking complementary colors for your Photoshop artwork, you can request a different Color Picker (one that looks more like a traditional color wheel), rather than using Photoshop's standard Color Picker (which isn't much help at all). This is done in the Photoshop menu (in Mac OS X), under General Preferences (in Windows, the Preferences can be found under the Edit menu). At the top of the General Prefs dialog, you'll see a pop-up menu for Color Picker. By default, it's set to Adobe. If you're using Windows, you can switch it to the standard Windows Color Picker. If you're on a Macintosh, you can choose to use Apple's Color Picker (actually, there's a host of different Color Pickers on the Mac, including CMYK, RGB, Crayon, and HSV). Apple's HSV Picker gives you a visual color wheel that makes picking complementary colors a breeze.

COLOR COMBINATIONS AFFECT SIZE AND PROPORTION

 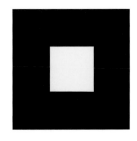

One thing to keep in mind when choosing color combinations is how different colors, and the balance between the colors themselves, affect how we perceive them. For example: Take a yellow square and place it over a white background. Now, take the same size square and place it over a black background. The square on the black background will appear to be smaller, even though the squares are exactly the same size. It's just how we perceive the color combination together. Remember that darker colors tend to look heavier and may overpower lighter colors. Along the same lines, when you place white text or reverse text over a black background, the text appears bold. It's one of those funky eyes-playing-tricks-on-you sort of things.

   USE TIGHT CROPPING TO SPICE UP IMAGES

We've all had those times when we're given less-than-spectacular photographic images to work with. It's your client's son or daughter, or maybe a really bad snapshot of a boring showroom or storefront. Here's a quick tip to give unimpressive photos a cool, hip, new look: Simply

use the Crop tool to tightly crop the image. You may even try rotating the image slightly, to give it that hip look. I know, it's really a no-brainer, but it does add a little pizzazz to boring images.

DETERMINING THE LENGTH OF A CAST SHADOW

One of the most commonly asked questions about cast shadows is, "How long or short do I make them?" We could get into a long and involved explanation, describing different lighting situations, such as single or multiple light sources, and viewing the subject from a bird's-eye perspective, blah, blah, blah…but we won't get into all that. After all, this is a quick tips book, so we'll oversimplify the answer just a bit.

What it comes down to is this: The length of the shadow is determined by the vertical position of the light source. For example, if the light source is directly above an object, it would hardly cast any shadow at all (see the illustration upper left), but if it was closer to the horizon line, it would cast a longer shadow (see the illustration, bottom left). In layman's terms: the higher the light source, the shorter the shadow; the lower the light source, the longer the shadow.

ADD A POINT OF REFERENCE TO CONVEY SIZE

If you're using Photoshop to "fool the eye," here are two tips for making objects look dramatically larger than they really are. First, to convey a sense of size, the eye needs a point of reference. So, if you want to create some type that looks 50 feet tall, place a silhouette of a person (just the person, no background) beside the type, and use Free Transform to shrink him to less than 30% of the height of the type.

The second tip is to rasterize your type, then use Free Transform to add a perspective effect to make your type appear as though it's so tall that you (the person viewing the image) are looking up at it (called foreshortening). To add perspective using Free Transform, first press Command-T (PC: Control-T) to bring up Free Transform.

Then, Control-click (PC: Right-click) within the bounding box and a pop-up menu of transformations will appear. Choose Perspective from this list, then grab the upper right-hand corner point and drag inward to create the perspective. When it looks about right to you, press Return (PC: Enter) to lock in your transformation.

Speedy Gonzalez

LAYER TIPS →

Speedy Gonzalez

layer tips

they're unimportant—they totally are. But when you say it—"layer tips"—it just doesn't have enough oomph! This chapter name needs more oomph! By the way, as an aside, if you look up the word "oomph" in the 2003 Webster's Abridged Dictionary, Oxford Version, for the actual definition, it's "A bulkiness or powerful quality that is brought on by most chapter heads, with the notable exception of 'Layer Tips'." Hey, I'm not making this stuff up. Those Webster guys are serious (especially the one who had his own show and was friends with Michael Jackson).

ALMOST A BUILT-IN FLATTENING SHORTCUT

I say "almost" because it works "almost" all the time. If you have a multi-layered file and want to quickly flatten it, you can usually press Shift-Command-E (PC: Shift-Control-E). The only time it doesn't work is when you have a hidden layer, because what you're pressing is the new keyboard shortcut for Merge Visible. If all your layers are visible, it flattens them, but if even one layer is hidden, it won't merge all the layers, only the visible ones. So you can use this "almost" all of the time.

  ## JUMP TO ANY LAYER JUST BY CLICKING IN YOUR IMAGE

You can jump to any layer in your document without going to the Layers palette. Press "v" to switch to the Move tool. Now, press-and-hold the Command key (PC: Control key), and click on an object on a layer in your image that you want, and you'll instantly jump to that layer.

TURNING YOUR LAYERS INTO SEPARATE DOCUMENTS

If you have a multi-layered document and want to turn each layer into its own separate document, just go under the File menu, under Scripts, and choose Export Layers to Files.

   OPENING LAYERED FILES WITHOUT ALL THE LAYERS

If you have a large multi-layered file, you know it can take a while to open, and that's fine—it's part of working with large files. But sometimes you're not going to actually work on the file, and you just want to open it, take a quick look at it, and then close it (maybe you just want to see if it's the version of the file you're looking for). So why waste time opening a huge multi-layered file if you just want to take a quick look? Well, you don't have to—just go under the File menu, choose Open, and navigate to the layered file, but before you click the Open button, hold Shift-Option (PC: Shift-Alt). By holding those two keys down before you choose Open, it opens a flattened version of your layered file. Pretty darn slick.

MISSING YOUR BACKGROUND LAYER? HERE'S THE FIX

If you're opening new documents and they don't have a Background layer, there's a reason (of course there's a reason; everything has a reason; we just happen to know what it is). The reason is that you've selected the Transparent option in the New document dialog. That seems like a reasonable thing to do; everybody wants transparency, right? However, what it tells Photoshop is "Don't worry about creating a Background layer." To get Background layers again, the next time you're in the New dialog, under Background Contents, make sure you choose White, and from then on, you'll have Background layers in your documents.

   AVOIDING THE LAYER MENU

Once you've applied a Layer Style to a layer, if you need to access some related commands that are in the Layer menu, you don't need to go up to the menu bar and go digging through the submenus. Instead, Control-click (PC: Right-click) on the little "*f*" icon that appears to the right of your layer's name in the Layers palette. A pop-up menu will appear with most of the Layer Style menu commands right at your fingertips—without the searching and digging through menus.

LOCK ALL THOSE LAYERS IN JUST ONE CLICK

You can lock all of your linked layers at once by choosing Lock All Linked Layers from the Layers palette's pop-down menu. They'll kick and scratch for a while, but they'll eventually calm right down.

TOGGLE THROUGH THE BLEND MODES

When I'm struggling to get just the right effect by changing the layer Blend Modes, it's great to be able to rotate through each mode without having to go back to the Blend Mode pop-down menu every time. To do this, simply switch to the Move tool, then press Shift-+ (plus sign). Every time you press it, it goes to the next Blend Mode.

HIDE YOUR OTHER LAYERS IN THE BLINK OF AN EYE

To hide an individual layer, click on the Eye icon in the first column next to that layer in the Layers palette. To make the layer visible again, click on the spot where the Eye icon used to be. If you want to keep one layer visible and hide all the others, hold the Option key (PC: Alt key) and click on the Eye icon beside the layer you want to keep visible. To make the other layers visible again, repeat the process.

WHY DRAGGING AND DROPPING STYLES ROCKS!

You probably already know that you can apply Styles to an image from the Styles palette, and you may even know that rather than just clicking on them, you can drag-and-drop these Styles right from the palette straight onto your current layer. But what's the advantage of dragging and dropping? Isn't it actually harder to drag-and-drop, rather than just clicking once? The advantage is that you can drag-and-drop styles to *any* layer, not just your currently active layer. You can also drag-and-drop effects between different open documents.

APPLYING LAYER STYLES TO YOUR BACKGROUND LAYER

How do you apply a Layer Style to your Background layer? You can't. That is, unless you double-click on your Background layer. This brings up the New Layer dialog where you can rename your Background layer, and when you do, it turns into a regular layer. Now you can apply Layer Styles to your heart's content. Want an even faster way? Just hold the Option key (PC: Alt key) and double-click. Then you won't get the dialog at all—it will just convert it into a new layer named Layer 0.

TURN YOUR LAYER COMPS INTO THEIR OWN DOCS

If you're using Layer Comps to compare different layouts within the same image, you can share these comps with people not on your network (or without access to your computer) by creating a separate document for each Layer Comp. This makes it easier to e-mail them, and easier for your recipient to view them. Luckily, you don't have to do this all manually; just go under the File menu, under Scripts, and choose Layer Comps to Files.

MORE CONTROL OVER BLENDS: ADVANCED BLENDING

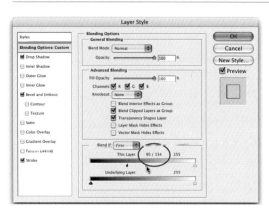

Using Blend Modes is a great way to get the layer you're on to interact with the layers beneath it. The only problem is you don't have much control over these Blend Modes—they either look the way you want them to, or they don't. They're pretty much an "on" or "off" tool. If you're looking for that next level of control over how layers interact with each other, you need the advanced Blending Options. These are found by double-clicking on the layer thumbnail in the Layers palette. What appears onscreen looks like the Layer Style dialog (and in fact, it is), but if you look closely, you'll see two bars with sliders giving you control over how your layered images interact. Here's another quick tip: If you hold the Option key (PC: Alt key) before you drag one of the sliders, it will split the slider in two, which gives you smoother transitions and more usable blend effects.

   INSTANT OPACITY CHANGE

Any time you want to change the Opacity of the layer you're currently working on, just switch to the Move tool and press a number key on your keyboard: 4 = 40% Opacity, 5 = 50% Opacity, etc. If you want an exact percentage, such as 52%, then type in 52 (note: you have to type quickly, or you'll get 50%, then 20%).

140 **CHAPTER 7** • Layer Tips

COPY A LAYER IN THE SAME LOCATION IN ANOTHER DOCUMENT

To make a copy of your current layer and have it appear in the exact same location in a different Photoshop document, Control-click (PC: Right-click) on the layer in the Layers palette that you want to copy, and choose Duplicate Layer. When the Duplicate Layer dialog appears, choose the Destination from the Document pop-up menu, and click OK.

   MOVING MULTIPLE LAYERS FROM DOCUMENT TO DOCUMENT

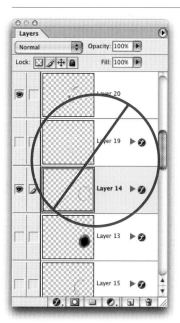

Want to move more than one layer at a time from one document to another? It's easy, as long as you know where to drag from. First, link your layers together, then make sure that you drag your layer from within your document itself, rather than trying to drag the layer from the Layers palette. Dragging a layer from the Layers palette to another document is fine, as long as you only want to drag one layer at a time.

CENTERING DRAGGED LAYERS THE EASY WAY

When dragging a layer from one document to another, the object will appear in the new document at the point your cursor was when you released the mouse button. If you'd prefer that the layer appear perfectly centered within the other document, just hold the Shift key as you drag, and when you release the mouse button, the object will be perfectly centered.

EASIER DROP SHADOW ANGLE ADJUSTMENTS

If you're creating a drop shadow using Photoshop's built-in Layer Styles, rather than setting the Distance and Angle numerically, you can adjust it visually. Just move your cursor outside the dialog right into your image, click on the shadow itself, and drag it where you'd like it.

LAYER NAVIGATION SHORTCUT

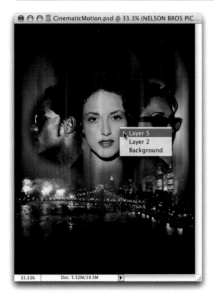

If you're working on a large, multi-layered document, you can jump to the layer you want by Control-clicking (PC: Right-clicking) over a portion of the image. A pop-up menu will appear with a list of the layers beneath the point where you clicked your cursor. To make one of those layers the active layer, just choose it from the list. It's important to note that if there aren't any layers beneath where you're Control-clicking (or the layers are transparent where you're clicking), the only layer that will appear in the pop-up menu is the Background layer.

SUPER-FAST LAYER COPIES

To instantly duplicate your current layer, just press Command-J (PC: Control-J). This also works if you want to duplicate just a portion of a layer. First, use the selection tool of your choice and make a selection of the area you want to duplicate. Now press Command-J (PC: Control-J), and that's all folks. Wait, what if you want to cut out the selected area from your current layer and put it up onto its own layer (so rather than just duplicating the selected area, you're cutting from the layer, and putting it onto another)? Then press Shift-Command-J (PC: Shift-Control-J) instead. This works great if you want to take the contents of your Background layer and put them onto it their own separate layer, without deleting the Background layer. Here's how it works: Press Command-A (PC: Control-A) to Select All, then press Shift-Command-J (PC: Shift-Control-J) to cut the background image out and put it on its own layer, above the now blank Background layer.

INSTANT LAYER ALIGNMENT

Aligning layers in Photoshop is easy. Just link the layers you want to align, then switch to the Move tool. In the Options Bar, you'll see icons for aligning horizontally, vertically, and to the left, right, and center, plus icons for equally distributing the spacing of your layered objects.

  SEPARATION ANXIETY: PUT A LAYER STYLE ON A SEPARATE LAYER

When you apply a Layer Style to a layer, you've done just that—applied a Style to a layer, and that Style is married to that layer. However, if you'd like to edit your effect separately from the layer, you can ask Photoshop to take the Layer Style and put it on its own separate layer (or layers if necessary). To do this, go under the Layer menu, under Layer Style, and choose Create Layers. Your effect will now appear on its own layer beneath your current layer. Note: If you apply a bevel effect, it will create multiple separate layers.

LAYER EFFECTS REMOVAL SPEED TIP

If you want to remove all the Layer Effects applied to a particular layer, don't drag them all into the Trash one by one. The fastest way is to simply drag the word "Effects" right into the Trash icon at the bottom of the Layers palette, and all the effects go right along with it.

   SHAPES WITHOUT THE SHAPE LAYER

If you use Photoshop's Shape tools, by default they create a Shape layer (which is basically a layer filled with your Foreground color, with a clipping path in the shape of your shape, if that makes any sense). We've had loads of e-mails from users asking us, "Do I have to have that funky Shape layer? Can't I just have the shape without the layer and clipping path?" Absolutely! When you choose one of the Shape tools, look up in the Options Bar and on the far left you'll see three icons. Click on the third icon from the left and you'll get just the shape—no Shape layer, no paths, no kidding.

COLOR-CODING MADE EASY

In Photoshop you can color-code layers and layer sets for quick visual identification. One way to do this is to bring up the Layer Properties dialog (from the Layers palette's pop-up menu) and choose your colors from a pop-up menu. But there's a much faster way—at least if you know this shortcut: Control-click (PC: Right-click) on the Eye icon next to the layer you want to color-code, and a pop-up menu of colors will appear where you can choose the shade you'd like.

   CAN'T PAINT ON A LAYER? HERE'S WHY

If you try and use one of Photoshop's paint tools to paint on a layer but Photoshop gives you the international symbol for "no you're not!", it's probably caused by one of two reasons: (1) You're trying to paint on a Type layer. Photoshop only allows one thing on Type layers—type! If you need to paint on a Type layer, you must first rasterize it (which converts it from an editable Type layer into a regular image layer). (2) The other reason is probably that the layer has been "locked" for painting. Look up in the top of the Layers palette and uncheck either the box that looks like a paintbrush or the one with the padlock (which Locks All).

SPEED UP PHOTOSHOP BY MERGING LAYERS

Every time you add a layer to Photoshop, it adds quite a bit of file size to your image. The larger your file size, the slower Photoshop goes. If you're creating a document that has lots of layers, before long, your file size is going to get pretty huge. One way to keep things lean and mean is to merge any layers that don't need to be separate. You do this by clicking on the topmost layer in the Layers palette, and then pressing Command-E (PC: Control-E). This merges the current layer with the layer directly beneath it. Think of it this way—every time you merge two layers, your file size drops and Photoshop gets faster. It's like a keyboard shortcut that adds more horsepower.

   ## LAYER SET SUPER-SPEED TIP

Want a quicker way to create a Layer Set? Link all the layers you want to include in this new set, then hold the Option key (PC: Alt key) and from the Layers palette's pop-down menu choose New Set From Linked. This will create a brand-new set consisting of all of your linked layers.

SAVE ROOM IN YOUR LAYERS PALETTE

This is a quick little tip for keeping your Layers palette shorter and more manageable. When you apply Layer Styles to your layers, each effect is listed separately in the Layers palette by default. If you apply five or six effects to one layer, it takes up a ton of room in your palette, and before you know it, you're scrolling farther and farther down the palette. To have it take up dramatically less space, collapse the effects in the palette by clicking on the down-facing triangle next to the little "*f*" icon to the right of the layer's name in the Layers palette. You can expand this list of effects anytime by clicking in the same spot.

CAN'T WE ALL JUST HAVE THE SAME STYLE?

Want to apply a Style that's on one layer to a bunch of other layers? It's easy (if you know the trick). Just link all the layers that you want to have that same Style, then go under the Layer menu, under Layer Style, and choose Copy Layer Style. Then, go under that same

menu again and choose Paste Layer Style To Linked, and your copied Style(s) will instantly paste to every linked layer.

   ## LAYER PALETTE NAVIGATION SPEED TIPS

The less you need to be in the Layers palette, the better (at least when it comes to speed), so here are some shortcuts you'll want to know: To jump to the bottom layer in the palette, press Shift-Option-Left Bracket ([) (PC: Shift-Alt-Left Bracket). To jump to the top of the layer stack, press Shift-Option-Right Bracket (]) (PC: Shift-Alt-Right Bracket). To move your current layer down one layer at a time, press Command-Left Bracket (PC: Control-Left Bracket). To move it up one layer at a time, press Command-Right Bracket (PC: Control-Right Bracket). To switch to the layer beneath your current layer, press Option-Left Bracket (PC: Alt-Left Bracket). To switch to the Layer above your current layer, press Option-Right Bracket (PC: Alt-Right Bracket).

QUICK-COPY YOUR LAYER MASK

If you've applied a Layer Mask to an image, you can duplicate that Layer Mask and apply it to another layer fairly easily. Start by clicking on the layer where you want this Layer Mask to appear. Then, click directly on the Layer Mask thumbnail that you want to copy and drag it down to the Layer Mask icon at the bottom of the Layers palette. When you do this, it creates an exact copy on your new layer.

SELECT EVERYTHING ON YOUR LAYER IN ONE CLICK

If you have a layer that contains many objects, you can put a selection around every object on that layer by holding the Command key (PC: Control key) and clicking on the Layer's name in the Layers palette. This is ideal in situations where you have an object that is heavily feathered or has a flattened drop shadow. If you use this trick, it will look like it only selects the most opaque portion of the image, but when you move it, you'll find it has selected every pixel on the layer, including the soft-edged pixels—it won't leave anything behind.

VIEW YOUR LAYER MASK AS A RUBYLITH

If you want to view your Layer Mask by itself (rather than how the Layer Mask affects your overall image), hold the Option key (PC: Alt key) and click directly on the Layer Mask thumbnail in the Layers palette. This will display just the Mask itself. You can also view the Layer Mask like a Rubylith (a red overlay used in traditional masking) by pressing the Backslash key (\) on your keyboard.

   SELECTING JUST ONE OBJECT ON A LAYER

If you have multiple objects on the same layer (like a few words of type that have already been rasterized) and you want to select just one item on that layer (for example, you want to put a selection around one letter so you can move it independently of the rest of the letters), here's how: Use the Lasso tool to draw a very loose selection around the object. Hold the Command key (PC: Control key), and then press the Up Arrow key once and the Down Arrow key once. The entire object will become perfectly selected without disturbing anything else on the layer. Now you can move it, edit it, or tweak it separately because it is now a "floating selection."

KEEP LAYER STYLES FROM AFFECTING NEW WORK

As you know, when you apply a Layer Style to a layer, it affects the entire layer. For example, if you apply a drop shadow to a layer, everything you do on that layer will have the same drop shadow applied to it. But what if you've applied a drop shadow and you want that shadow to remain, but you want to do other things on that layer without having an automatic drop shadow added to them? Here's what to do: Create a new blank layer by clicking on the Create a New Layer icon at the bottom of the Layers palette, and drag this new layer beneath your layer with the drop shadow. Click on your drop shadow layer (to make it the active layer), and then press Command-E (PC: Control-E) to merge it with the blank layer directly beneath it. This will remove the active effect from the layer (so it no longer applies a drop shadow to new things on the layer), but it will leave the shadow effect on the objects that were there before the merge.

UN-FILLING FOR FUN AND PROFIT

Back in Photoshop 7.0, Adobe brought a once-buried command front and center when they added the "Fill" opacity to the Layers palette. This isn't your average everyday fill. No sir. This is a special freaky fill that works only when you've applied a Layer Style to a layer. To see it in action (and immediately understand its power), create some text, and then apply a drop shadow. Lower the regular Opacity of this layer, and you'll notice that both your type and the shadow fade at the same time. Now raise it back up to 100%. Then lower the Fill amount (in the Layers palette) and you'll notice that the type fades away, but the drop shadow stays at 100%. Ahhhhhh. Makes you stop and think, doesn't it?

   OPACITY SLIDER SPEED TIPS

If you're using the Opacity slider in the Layers palette, you can control this slider (which frankly is a bit awkward to control with your mouse) by using the Arrow keys on your keyboard. Here's how: Click on the right-facing triangle next to the Opacity field, then use the Left and Right Arrow keys to move 1% at a time. If you hold the Shift key, you'll move 10% at a clip.

SECRET OPACITY SEE-THROUGH PART OF A LAYER TIP

This is a pretty wild tip—how to make just one part of a layer have a lower opacity. We know it sounds impossible, but this is totally cool. Start by making a selection on any area of the layer that you want to become transparent, while the rest of the layer remains at 100%. Then go under the Edit menu and choose Fill. When the Fill dialog appears, from the Blend Mode pop-up menu choose Clear. Then lower the Opacity of the fill to whatever percentage you'd like, then click OK and voilà—part of your layer has opacity, while the rest remains at 100%. Majorly cool! (Note: You have to think in reverse here. Clear set to 100% Opacity will make the selected area completely transparent.) Wait, what if you decide later that you want to "fill it back in"? Here's how: Just start making copies of your layer, and as you do, you'll see the transparency disappear. You may have to make five or more copies, but son of a gun if it doesn't work. When it looks right, hide all but those copied layers, and from the Layers palette's pop-down menu, choose Merge Visible.

SKIPPING THE LAYER COMP DIALOG

When you create a new Layer Comp, you're always faced with the New Layer Comp dialog so you'll have the opportunity to make any notes about the comp, or name it if you like. However, I find that most of the time I just want a new comp, not the dialog (after all, if I want to name the version, I can just click right on its name in the Layer Comps palette. In fact, the only time I want the dialog is when I want to add a comment, which is rare). So to skip the New Layer Comp dialog, just Option-click (PC: Alt-click) the Create New Layer Comp icon at the bottom of the Layer Comps palette, and you'll just get the comp—not the dialog.

I've got to be honest with you, I'm not sure you really need this chapter, so let's do a little quiz to start things off, and if for some reason you

Speed Freak

troubleshooting tips

fail this impromptu quiz, then you'll have to read the chapter. Pass, and you jump straight to Chapter 9. Ready? Begin (you have 12 minutes for the first segment).

Question One: If Photoshop crashes while copying a 50-MB file into Clipboard memory, do you (a) pack up your computer, call Billie Joe MacAllister and ask him to meet you at the Tallahatchie bridge; (b) completely disrobe, sit cross-legged on the floor while burning candles around the Photoshop product box; (c) press Shift-Alt-Control-Delete-Tilde-Tab-Escape-Enter-Option-F15-Backslash, proving you have eleven fingers; or (d) all of the above?

Answer: It was a trick question. Obviously, the real answer would have been "b," except you never, never dare to have an open flame anywhere near your Photoshop product box. Sorry, grasshopper—turn the page and start reading.

THE REAPPEARING/DISAPPEARING BRUSH TIP

This one gets more people because it's a feature that acts like a bug. Has this ever happened to you? You're working in Photoshop, you're using the Brush tool, and everything seems fine. But a little later in your session, you get the Brush tool again, and it no longer displays the size of the currently selected brush tip. Instead, it displays a little crosshair cursor. So you go to the Preferences menu and choose Display and Cursors, and sure enough, you've got "Brush Size" chosen as your preference, but for some strange reason, it's not showing your brush size; it's showing that stupid crosshair. Here's the problem: Check your Caps Lock key. It's turned on, and turning it on changes your Brush cursor from displaying brush size to displaying the crosshair. This is actually a feature to be used when you need to see the precise center of your brush. The problem is it's assigned to the Caps Lock key, so every time you turn on Caps Lock when you're working with type, you just temporarily switched your Brush cursor. Does Adobe need to find a better key for this feature/bug? You betcha! Will it happen? Not as far as I know.

   GET PRINT RESOLUTION FROM YOUR DIGITAL CAMERA IMAGES

Problem: You imported an image from your digital camera and although the physical dimensions of the image are rather large, the resolution shows up as only 72 ppi. How can you get enough resolution to print this image? Solution: Go under the Image menu and choose Image Size. Turn off Resample Image, then in the Resolution field, type in the resolution you need for the specific device you'll be printing to. When you do this, Photoshop will automatically input the Height and Width

that would result from using that resolution (the image size will definitely be smaller—the higher the resolution needed, the smaller the physical dimensions of your image). All you have to do is click OK and Photoshop will do the math, creating an image in the new smaller size, with the new higher resolution. The good news is that by doing it this way, there's absolutely *no* loss of quality to the file whatsoever.

HOW TO USE RGB FILTERS ON GRAYSCALE IMAGES

If you're working on grayscale images, you'll find there are some Photoshop filters that won't work (they're grayed out, so you can't access them). Of course, it's always the really cool filters, such as Lens Flare and Lighting Effects, that are grayed out. But don't be dismayed (in fact, be "mayed") because you can still use those filters—just switch to RGB mode, run the filters, then switch back to Grayscale mode. It won't affect the color of your image because, well, there is no color—you're working on a grayscale image. Switching to RGB doesn't suddenly pour color onto your image; your grayscale image will still look grayscale in RGB. When you switch back to Grayscale mode (after applying the filters), you'll get a warning asking, "Discard color information?" You can safely click OK, because after all, there was no color to begin with.

STOP THE CROP SNAPPING

Problem: When you're trying to crop an image using the Crop tool, your cropping border tries to snap to the edges of your document window. This might also be happening when drawing large Marquee selections as well. Solution: Press Shift-Command-; (PC: Shift-Control-;), which is the shortcut for turning off this snapping. The only downside is it turns off all snapping (like snap to guides, snap to rulers, etc.). If you just want the Crop snapping (or Marquee snapping) off, go under the View menu, under Snap To, and choose Document Bounds, and your tools will no longer try and snap to your, well, document bounds.

LET'S DO THE TEXT WARP AGAIN

I get more people than you can "stick a shake at" asking me about this problem. If you go to use Photoshop's Warped Text function, you might get a warning that states, "Could not complete your request because the type layer uses a faux bold style." A faux bold style? What in the wide world of sports is that? Actually, it's a feature of Photoshop (that was introduced back in Photoshop 5.0) that lets you create a fake (faux) bold or italic type style for fonts that don't really have a bold or italic type style. It's toggled on/off in the Character palette's pop-up menu. In Photoshop 7.0, Adobe added the option in the warning dialog to "Remove attribute and continue." All you have to do is click OK to remove the faux bold and now you can Warp your text. Life is good.

   UNLOCKING THE BACKGROUND LAYER

Can't move the Background layer? That's because back in Photoshop 6, Adobe locked the Background layer from movement. That wouldn't be so bad, except that if you look at the top of the Layers palette, you can see that "Yup, the checkbox to lock movement is turned on," but the frustrating part is that it's also grayed out, so you can't simply uncheck it to unlock it. The only way around this is to double-click on the Background, which brings up the New Layer dialog. Click OK, and your Background layer becomes Layer 0 and is unlocked. Now you can move it.

TRIMMING YOUR PLUG-INS FOR FASTER STARTUP

If Photoshop takes forever to load on startup, there may be a good reason. One of the things that takes a long time to load are Photoshop's plug-ins. The more you have, the longer it takes. These plug-ins also eat up RAM, so when it comes to plug-ins, fewer plug-ins means faster Photoshop. One way around this is to create a custom folder of just the plug-ins that you use on a daily basis. That way, only the plug-ins you really need will load. Here's how: Simply create a new folder, and name it something like "slim plug-ins" or "Slim Whitman plug-ins" or even perhaps "hair plug-ins." Next, make a copy of just the plug-ins you want in this set and put them in your newly named folder. To make this your active plug-in set, just hold Shift-Command (PC: Shift-Control) while launching Photoshop, and a dialog will appear asking you to choose which plug-ins folder you want to use. Choose your "slim plug-ins" folder and click OK, and that set will load from now on. If you ever want the full default set of plug-ins to load instead, just hold the same keyboard command and choose "Plug-ins" as your set to load.

   MAKING YOUR COLOR PRINTOUTS MATCH YOUR MONITOR

Are the images that come out of your color inkjet printer looking much different from what they looked like onscreen in Photoshop? Are the images oversaturated and do they just look unnatural? There could be a host of reasons, but one of the first things to check is which color mode you're in when you're printing. Many people switch to CMYK mode before printing their image, because, after all, their printer has four inks: cyan, magenta, yellow, and black. The problem is, you're not printing color separations, where you get four sheets from one image—one cyan, one magenta, one yellow, and one black. Instead, you're printing a composite image (one page with all the colors, rather than four separate sheets). So in most cases, you should stay in RGB mode for results that will better match your screen. Most color inkjets produce much more accurate results when you're using RGB images (the printers actually do a special RGB-to-CMYK conversion in the printer driver to make use of the CMYK inks, but if you do it first, all hell breaks loose). Not sure if this is true? Try a test on your printer: Print the same image twice—once in RGB mode, then convert the exact same image to CMYK and try again. In just a few seconds, you'll have the definitive answer.

DO YOU HAVE ENOUGH RAM? ASK PHOTOSHOP

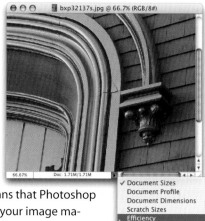

Not sure if you have enough RAM? Just ask Photo-shop. Believe it or not, it can tell you. Here's how: Open a document that's indicative of the type of image you normally work on. Work on the image, doing typical stuff, for about 10 minutes. In the bottom left-hand corner of your document window, just to the right of the current document magnification readout, is the Info box. By default, it's set to display your document's file size, but if you click-and-hold on the right-facing triangle to the right of it, a pop-up list of options will appear. Choose Efficiency. If the percentage shown is 100%, you're gold, baby! That means that Photoshop is running at peak efficiency, because 100% of the time your image ma-nipulations are being handled in RAM. If the efficiency number shown is, say, 75%, this means that 25% of the time, Photoshop ran out of RAM and had to use free hard drive space to make up for it, which means Photoshop ran *much* slower 25% of the time. An efficiency of 75% is pretty much as low as you want it to go. If it shows anything less than 75%, it's time to buy more RAM. Pronto!

   GETTING BETTER EPS PREVIEWS

Problem: The image looked great in Photoshop, but now that you've converted it to CMYK, saved the file as a TIFF, and placed it into QuarkXPress, InDesign, PageMaker, etc., the image looks awful—way oversaturated and totally whacked. Reason: The preview of CMYK TIFFs just looks like that, so don't freak out—if it looked right in Photoshop, it should print fine. Okay, what if you saved the file as an EPS, and when you place the image into your page layout app, the color of the image looks okay, but it's not crisp and clear, but pixelated. Reason: By default, the preview embedded within EPS images is a lame 256-color preview. Solution: In the EPS Options dialog, under Preview, choose JPEG. That way, it sends a 24-bit, full-color preview, rather than the lame 256-color preview.

THE KILLER TROUBLESHOOTING TIP: DELETING THE PREFERENCES

This is probably the most important tip in this entire chapter because if something goes wrong in Photoshop, almost regardless of what it is, deleting Photoshop's preferences file will usually fix it. In fact, if you call Adobe tech support, this is usually the first thing they'll tell you to try when you're having problems, so you might as well beat them to the punch. All you have to do is find the

preferences file, delete it, then (and this is key) restart Photoshop, and the program will automatically build a new factory-fresh set of preferences, and chances are that'll fix the problem. The only hard part of this repair scenario is actually finding the preferences themselves, which apparently were hidden by the same person who hid Jimmy Hoffa, so they're not easy to find. Here's where to look:

Windows 2000:
C:\Documents and Settings\<username>\ApplicationData\AdobePhotoshop\CS\Adobe Photoshop CS Settings

Windows XP:
C:\Documents and Settings\<username>\ApplicationData\Adobe\Photoshop\CS\Adobe Photoshop CS Settings

Macintosh OS X v. 10.2-10.3:
Users\<username>\Library\Preferences\Adobe Photoshop CS Settings\Adobe Photoshop CS Prefs

GET BACK YOUR BACKGROUND LAYER

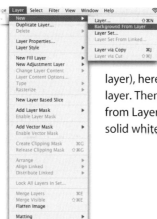

Lost your Background layer? It happens. It's heartbreaking, but it happens. If you suddenly find yourself staring at a Layers palette and there's no Background layer (chances are you accidentally converted your Background layer into a regular layer), here's how to get a Background layer again: Create a new blank layer. Then, go under the Layer menu, under New, and choose Background from Layer, and Photoshop will take your new blank layer and create a solid white Background layer at the bottom of your layer stack.

EXPANDING RECTANGULAR SELECTIONS

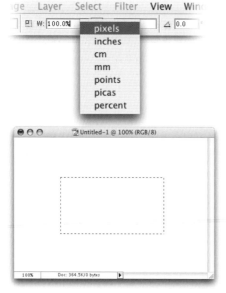

If you've ever tried to expand a rectangular selection by more than five or six pixels, you know what happens. The crisp, sharp-edged corners that you start off with become rounded. Here's the fix: Don't use the Expand submenu. First, make your selection and press Command-T (PC: Control-T) to bring up the Free Transform bounding box. Go up to the Options Bar and Control-click (PC: Right-click) in the Width and Height fields to change the measurements from percent to pixels. Now, simply add the amount of pixels you want to expand to the existing number. For example: If the field reads 110 pixels, and you want to expand it by 10 pixels, enter 120 pixels in the field and press Enter to apply the transformation. Don't forget to change both the Width and Height fields. That's it—perfectly expanded corners.

FIXING THE "ROUNDED CORNERS" SELECTION PROBLEM

Ever have this happen? You draw a selection with the Rectangular Marquee tool (the square/rectangular selection tool) and the corners of your selection are rounded, rather than nice and straight? This happens to a lot of people, especially if they've been drinking. If you haven't been drinking but you're suffering from rounded-corner selections, look up in the Options Bar, and you'll see a field for Feather. Chances are there's some number other than "0" in this field, and what's happening is every time you draw a selection with that tool, it's automatically feathering (softening) the edge. What probably happened is you either intentionally (or accidentally) added a feather amount at some time, then later forgot to set it back to its default of zero. So to fix it, just highlight the field and type 0. Incidentally, this is a great Photoshop prank to play on coworkers, friends, soon-to-be-enemies, etc., because the Feather field is usually the last place they'll look.

   ## MAKING GLOBAL LIGHT WORK FOR YOU

Problem: You applied a drop shadow to an object on one layer, then later, you applied a bevel on another layer, but in the Bevel and Emboss dialog, when you go to change the angle of your bevel, you notice that the position of your drop shadow just moved as well. Reason: Adobe uses a feature (that acts like a bug) called Global Light. The idea behind it makes sense, yet we've never run into the scenario it was created for. The idea is this: You've created an image with lots of drop shadows, all casting in a particular direction. If the client saw your work and said, "Hey, instead of having the shadows go down and to the right, can we make all the shadows go up and to the left?" If that unlikely event ever occurred, you'd be set, because all you'd have to do is move one shadow and all the other shadows on other layers would move to the exact same angle. It's a great idea; it just never happens (okay, it's probably happened somewhere, once). Solution: In the Layer Style dialog, uncheck the Use Global Light box. Now you can move the angle of your current Layer Style separately from the rest of your image. Life is good once more.

CHAPTER 8 • Troubleshooting Tips **165**

FIND THE HIDDEN MAGNETIC PEN TOOL OPTIONS

I know what you're thinking—finding the Magnetic Pen tool options? I didn't even know there was a Magnetic Pen tool in the first place. Adobe has done a great job of hiding it, and in CS, its options are buried even deeper than before. For some reason they must hate this tool. Anyway, to get to the Magnetic Pen tool (the magnetic part means it snaps to well-defined edges to help you draw accurate paths around objects), you have to start by choosing the Freeform Pen tool from the Toolbox. Only then will the subterranean magnetic checkbox surface in the Options Bar.

However, to access the all-important "Magnetic Options" so you have a chance in hell of actually controlling this tool, you have to dig deeper into the underground world of CS to make these options bubble to the top. Click on the down-facing black triangle to the right of the Custom Shape tool icon in the Options Bar to reveal a pop-down menu few will ever see—the Freeform Pen Options. In this rarely viewed menu, you'll find a checkbox for "Magnetic," and clicking on it will bring the grayed-out Magnetic options to life, and open a treasure chest of newfound riches (also known as more boring options).

PRINTING SHADOWS OVER SOLID COLORS IN PAGE LAYOUT APPS

This is such a cool tip (I'm not sure it's a troubleshooting tip, but the concept causes so many problems that we thought we'd stick it here). The problem is this: How do you put an object (such as a chair, a clock, or some sort of silhouetted image) with a soft drop shadow over a colored background in your page layout application (such as QuarkXPress, InDesign, or Page-Maker)? Think about it. It's harder than it sounds. You can't use a clipping path, or it will clip off the soft edges, leaving an unsightly white edge. The ideal solution is to create the entire background in Photoshop and put your object and shadow over that background, and then export the whole shebang as one giant file into your page layout program. Unfortunately, oftentimes, because of the particular project you're working on, you simply can't do that. So how do you pull off this mini miracle? Create what's called a dithered shadow.

It's not hard, but it's kind of scary for most people. Here's how:

1. First, go under the Image menu and make a duplicate of your object image by choosing Duplicate.

2. Change your Foreground color to 40% gray, and then go to your object layer and press Shift-Option-Delete (PC: Shift-Alt-Backspace) to fill your object with gray. Apply a Gaussian Blur to make your 40% gray layer have soft edges (this will become your shadow).

3. Convert your RGB image into Grayscale mode by going under the Image menu, under Mode, and choosing Grayscale. When the dialog appears asking if you want to discard the color, click OK.

4. Now convert your Grayscale image to Bitmapped mode. When the Bitmap dialog appears, under Output enter 600 using pixels/inch and set the method to Diffusion Dither. Rename the file and save it in TIFF format.

5. Import your shadow into your page layout application, and then import your original Photoshop object (with a clipping path applied so you get just the object, not the white background surrounding it) and position it over your shadow where you'd like it (of course, be sure to position the shadow so that it extends outside your object and is clearly visible).

6. This is the critical (read scary) part of this process. In your page layout application, you *must* set this TIFF shadow to overprint the background (rather than knock out, like it normally would). This way, when you image the film at high resolution, the shadow will appear smooth and will overprint the background, looking like a soft shadow without the white halo. One reason this technique freaks people out is that onscreen, you still see the white pixels over your background in your page layout application, so it takes a leap of faith to print something that onscreen looks wrong. It's a gutsy technique, but people pull it off everyday. Tough people. Gutsy people. Mostly Marines.

● LET PHOTOSHOP REBUILD YOUR PREFS

If you need to delete Photoshop's current preferences file (which is a common "first-line-of-defense" troubleshooting move), you don't have to go digging around your drive. In CS, all you have to do is hold the Shift, Option, and Command keys (PC: Shift-Alt-Control) when you first launch Photoshop, and you'll be greeted with a dialog asking

you if you want to delete the Photoshop Settings File. If you do, click yes, and Photoshop will build a new factory-fresh set of preferences for you.

STOP THE "CLICK-AND-JUMP-TO-THAT-LAYER" BLUES

Problem: All of a sudden, every time you click on a layer with the Move tool, it jumps to that layer. Solution: Somehow you turned on a feature called Auto Select Layer, which lets you make a layer active by just clicking on it with the Move tool. To turn this feature off, click on the Move tool, and up in the Options Bar, turn off the checkbox for Auto Select Layer. Besides, you never really need to turn this feature on, because you can just hold the Command key (PC: Control key) and click on any layer.

FASTER APPLICATION SWITCHING

Do you often copy-and-paste images from Photoshop into other applications (such as FileMaker Pro, Word, etc.)? I'm not talking about importing a TIFF or EPS; I'm talking about copying the object, switching to another application, and pasting your copied image from the clipboard. You don't? Great, then we have a tip for you that will speed up your application-switching pretty dramatically. Go under the Photoshop menu, under Preferences, under General, and turn off the checkbox for Export Clipboard (in Windows, Preferences can be found under the Edit menu). Here's what's happening when it's turned on: Whatever you last copied in Photoshop gets transferred to your system's Clipboard memory when you switch to another application, just in case you want to paste it. If you have a large image in clipboard, you'll get a dialog with a status bar saying "Exporting Clipboard," and while it's there, you can only sit there and wait. Turn off that preference, and wait no more.

   ## WILL MORE RAM MAKE PHOTOSHOP RUN FASTER?

Problem: You added more RAM to your system and assigned more RAM to Photoshop, but it doesn't seem to run any faster. Reason: Adding RAM doesn't always make Photoshop run faster. It only works if you didn't have enough RAM to begin with. Adding RAM will only help to make your computer run as fast as it can, but it won't make your 800-MHz computer run at 801 MHz. For example, if you work on Web images and the average image you work on is 3 MB, you only need about 15 or 20 MB assigned to Photoshop to have it run at full speed. If you've got that, and add another 256 MB of RAM, Photoshop won't run any faster, because Photoshop only needs that 15 or 20 MB that you already had. Freaky.

DON'T USE CROP TO FIX BARREL DISTORTION

Problem: You're trying to fix barrel distortion that appears on a photo you're editing, but using the Crop tool's Perspective feature is a guessing game. You try the crop and it doesn't look right; you have to undo it, and guess again. Solution: Don't use the Crop tool's Perspective feature, even though it was specifically designed to address barrel distortion. Use the standard Free Transform tool instead, because with it, you get a live onscreen preview as you work, so fixing the distortion takes just a few seconds.

   ## GETTING SMALLER PHOTOSHOP FILES

Do your Photoshop .psd file sizes seem a little large? It may be because of a preference setting that makes Photoshop save a flattened version of your Photoshop image, along with your layered Photoshop file. Why does Photoshop do this? Because there's a slight possibility you might share this file with someone using Photoshop 2.5 (just like there's a slight possibility that Congress will vote to cut their own salaries), and Photoshop 2.5 didn't support layers, so it can't read your layered document. But because, by default, that flattened version is included in your layered file, guess what—2.5 can open the flattened image. What luck! Who cares? I'd rather have smaller file sizes all year long, and if you would too, go under the Photoshop menu (the Edit menu in Windows), under Preferences, under File Handling, then in the File Compatibility section, for Maximize PSD File Compatibility, change "Ask" to "Never." Think about this one for a minute and you'll wonder why this is turned on by default. Think about it for two minutes and you'll wonder why it's in Photoshop at all. Don't spend too much time on it, or you'll start to wonder who's the poor soul that's stuck on version 2.5.

● ● ● **HOW TO USE ACTIONS FROM THE WEB**

Problem: You downloaded an action from a Web site, but Photoshop doesn't seem to recognize it. How do you get it into Photoshop? Solution: First, make sure the action has the file extension .atn (which lets Photoshop know it's a Photoshop action). Go to the Actions palette and, under the palette's pop-down menu, choose Load Actions. Then, locate your action and click Load, and that action will appear under its own set in the Actions palette, where you can run it.

CoolText.atn

Speed
2

PREPRESS
TIPS

We're getting near the end of the book, and I'm growing tired. Dark figures dance across the windows like so many shadows gathering dust for the fall harvest (see,

Speed 2

image-correction and prepress tips

this is why they don't let me write chapter intros at 2:30 a.m. anymore). Originally, this chapter was going to be a catchall chapter—a place for all those tips that couldn't find a home by the end of the book, but as luck would have it, we had so many image-correction and prepress tips, they actually took over the catchall chapter by force.

Now, because we stuck these image-correction and prepress tips at the back of the book, does it mean that these tips aren't as good, aren't as important, or aren't as cool as the tips in all the other chapters? Yes, that's exactly what it means. These are the tips that just aren't worth a darn, so don't even waste your time reading them, because, frankly, I'm not sure how many of them really work. Oh, I'm sure one or two do, but at this point, I'm just making stuff up.

I know there are many new users of Photoshop that will be reading this book, so I think a description of the term "prepress" is in order. "Pre," as you know, means before, and "press" is derived from the Latin word meaning "to unwrinkle one's pants with an iron." So, basically, read this chapter before you wrinkle your pants.

GETTING MORE ACCURATE COLOR USING REPLACE COLOR

If you're using Replace Color (under the Image menu, under Adjustments) to select an area within your photo and replace it with a different color, the new color is pretty much an approximation, because you're dragging sliders, rather than input-ting the exact RGB or CMYK build you're looking for. In Photoshop CS, there's a way around this. Once you've selected the area of color you want to replace, click on the Color Swatch to the right of the sliders in the Replacement section (it wasn't there in previous versions). This brings up the Color Picker, where you can enter the exact RGB or CMYK values for your new color.

 CORRECTING HIGHLIGHTS? WATCH OUT FOR OPEN SHADOWS!

If you open the Shadow/Highlight command (found in the Image menu, under Adjustments) to open up the shadows in your photo, you're in good shape from the get-go because it automatically increases the shadow area by 50%. That's great, if that's what you're after. But what if you're trying to pull back the highlights in a photo? Shadow/Highlight doesn't know that and by default still opens up your shadows by 50%. The way to combat this is to immediately drag the Shadows slider all the way to the left when the dialog appears, so now you can just adjust (pull back) the highlights by dragging the Highlights slider to the right, which now affects just the highlights and not the shadows.

HOW TO HEAL ON A BLANK LAYER

One of the cornerstones of professional retouching is to always perform your retouches on their own separate layer. That way you never "bruise" (damage) the pixels of the original image. However, when using the Healing Brush in Photoshop 7, you really had no choice—you had to use it on the same layer. In Photoshop CS, you can heal to another layer. But first, there's a little setting you have to change. Get the Healing Brush from the Toolbox, then up in the Options Bar, turn on the checkbox for Use All Layers. Next, click on the Create a New Layer icon at the bottom of the Layers palette to create a new blank layer above your Background layer and do your "healing" there.

   ## BETTER HEALING WITH A CUSTOM BRUSH

I have to give credit for this incredible tip to NAPP member Stephanie Cole, who showed it to me after the Midnight Madness session at the PhotoshopWorld Conference & Expo in LA. She pointed out how you can get a real mottled-looking result sometimes when using the Healing Brush. However, she found that when you change the brush shape (by clicking on the brush thumbnail in the Options Bar) to a tall thin brush, it heals using a star-shaped stroke. This greatly reduces the mottling often associated with the Healing Brush, creating a smoother-looking, more natural retouch. My thanks to Stephanie for allowing me to share her very slick trick.

CREATING A CUSTOM SHADOW/HIGHLIGHT DEFAULT

By default, the Shadow/Highlight adjustment command decreases the shadows by 50%, but if you'd prefer to have Shadow/Highlight open flat (with no automatic shadow adjustment), you can set your own defaults. That way, you decide how much, and when, the shadows get opened. You do this by going under the Image menu, under Adjustments, choosing Shadow/Highlight, and then dragging the Shadows slider to 0%. Click on the Show More Options checkbox, and at the bottom of the expanded dialog click on the Save As Defaults button. That's it: Now you get to decide if the shadows get opened up, and how much, because everything's set flat.

GETTING BACK SHADOW/HIGHLIGHT'S FACTORY DEFAULTS

Don't ever be concerned about experimenting in Photoshop CS's amazing Shadow/Highlight feature—mess with the sliders all you want, because you can always get back to the factory default settings, even if you've overridden them by saving your own defaults. You do this within the Shadow/Highlight dialog by clicking on the Show More Options checkbox. Then, hold the Shift button, and you'll see the Save As Defaults button at the bottom of the expanded dialog change to the Reset Defaults button. Click it, and the factory defaults are back, baby!

HEALING WITH PRESSURE

If you're using a Wacom tablet and wireless pen with Photoshop, you've probably already uncovered the secret hiding place where Adobe tucked the pressure sensitivity controls (hint: they're in the Brushes palette), but if you want to use pressure sensitivity with the Healing Brush, it's in a totally different spot. To turn it on, click on the Healing Brush tool, then up in the Options Bar, click directly on the Brush Sample, and a menu will pop up (it's not the standard Brushes Picker). At the bottom of the menu, you'll see a pop-up for Size, where you can choose "Pen Pressure."

   CONTROL THE OPACITY OF YOUR HEALING PROCESS

I don't know if you've noticed, but Photoshop's Healing Brush doesn't have an option for controlling its opacity (the way the Clone Stamp, Brush, Eraser, and other tools have). But there is a workaround if you want to use the brush and have some control over its opacity. Just go ahead and use the brush first; then to lower the opac-

ity of your stroke, go under the Edit menu and choose Fade Healing Brush. When the Fade dialog appears, just lower the Opacity slider to the desired amount. It's a bit clunky, but it works.

SAY GOOD-BYE TO GRADIENT BANDING

If you've printed an image with a gradient in it, you're probably familiar with banding (a visible line where one color ends and the next starts, like bands of color, instead of a smooth transition from one color to the next). There's a very popular tip for getting rid of banding that's very effective for high-resolution imaging. Open the image in Photoshop and go under the Filter menu, under Noise, and choose Add Noise. When the Add Noise dialog appears, for Amount enter 2, for Distribution choose Gaussian, turn on the Monochromatic checkbox, and then click OK. You'll see a little bit of this noise when viewing the image onscreen, but when printed at high resolution, the noise disappears and hides the banding. We add noise to every gradient we create for just that reason.

   ## SHARPENING YOUR IMAGES LIKE A PRO

Just about every image that is brought into Photoshop, whether from a scanner, digital camera, CD-ROM, etc., needs to be sharpened. The undisputed tool for this task is Photoshop's Unsharp Mask filter. The only downside of using this filter is that getting the level of sharpening you'd like can sometimes cause color shifts and halos, and it can also accentuate dust or specs within the image. There are two ways around this, and what's great about these methods is they let you apply a higher level of sharpening without causing color shifts or other problems: (1) Convert your file from RGB mode to Lab Color. Then go to the Channels palette and click on the Lightness channel. Now apply the Unsharp Mask filter (twice if you need it), then switch back to RGB mode (don't worry, there's no harm in this RGB-to-Lab-to-RGB mode conversion). (2) If you're working on a CMYK image, apply the Unsharp Mask filter, then go under the Edit menu and choose Fade Unsharp Mask. When the Fade dialog appears, change the Fade Unsharp Mask mode to Luminosity and click OK (which pretty much does the same thing as method 1; it applies the sharpening to the luminance of the image, not the color).

FIVE TIPS FOR GETTING RID OF MOIRÉ PATTERNS

If you scanned an image that already has been printed in one form or another, you're bound to get a moiré pattern over your image (moiré patterns are a series of dots or spots that appear on your image). These spots are your scanner picking up the halftone screen that was applied when the image was printed.

Here are five quick tips for removing moiré patterns:

1. Go under the Filter menu, under Noise, and choose Despeckle. There are no numbers to input or sliders to adjust—it either works or it doesn't, but luckily, it works about 75% of the time. However, if you run Despeckle and it doesn't work, undo it. That's because Despeckle adds a slight blur to your entire image, and if it doesn't work, there's no sense in leaving that blur applied, eh?

2. Apply a 1-pixel or less Gaussian Blur. This will usually work if method 1 doesn't. Again, if this technique doesn't remove the moiré pattern, undo it to reduce unnecessary blurring.

3. Go under the Filter menu, under Noise, and choose Median. Enter 1 pixel and click OK. I know I'm sounding like a broken record, but if it doesn't work, undo it. You know why.

4. Reduce the resolution of your scan to twice the line screen it will be printed at. For example, if you scanned it at 300 dpi and you're going to print it at 100 line screen, lower the resolution of the file to 200 ppi and that'll probably do the trick. If this image is going to be used on the Web, when you lower the resolution to 72 ppi, that'll probably do it.

5. Lastly, try rescanning the image with the image rotated slightly on the scanner bed. This is a last resort, but if all else fails, this will probably do the trick. Once the image is in Photoshop, you'll have to straighten the scan, but at least the moiré pattern will be gone.

SCAN LINE ART AT THE RESOLUTION YOU NEED

If you're scanning black-and-white line art for reproduction in print, here are two quick tips that'll help you get better results:

1. Scan the line art image at the dpi you'll be printing it. This is the one time we break our long-standing "don't-scan-at-too-high-a-resolution" rule—but only when it comes to line art. If you're going to output your line art on a 600-dpi laser printer, scan it at 600 dpi. If you're going to output it to high-resolution film negs, scan it at 1,200 dpi (that's about as high as you'll need to go).

2. Scan your line art images in Grayscale mode. If you do, then you can apply filters such as the Unsharp Mask to help clean and define the lines, and you can use Levels to brighten the white areas.

Note: If you scan in Bitmap mode, you won't be able to use these two important line art cleanup tips, because they're not supported in Bitmap mode.

   USING THE HIGH PASS FILTER FOR SHARPENING

There's a sharpening technique that's really gaining popularity that works especially well on images with lots of well-defined edges (such as buildings, cars, furniture, etc.). It's actually a layer technique combined with a filter, but it's very easy (and often very effective) to apply. Start by duplicating the Background layer of the image you want to sharpen. Then, go under the Filter menu, under Other, and choose High Pass. When the High Pass dialog appears, enter a Radius of 1.5 pixels (a good starting point) and click OK to apply the filter. It will change your image into a gray mess, but don't sweat it (yet). To bring the sharpening into your image, change the Blend mode of this layer to Soft Light. The gray will disappear, and the edges of your image will appear sharper. You can also try the Hard Light mode to increase the sharpening effect. Still not enough? Make a copy of the layer for a multiplying effect. Is one copy not enough sharpening, but two are too much? You can control the sharpening amount in two ways: (1) Switch between Soft Light and Hard Light, or (2) lower the Opacity setting of the layer to dial in just the right amount of sharpening.

SPOT COLOR GRADIENT FILM SAVER

If you're creating a gradient using a spot color that fades to white, to make sure your gradient appears just on the spot separation plate, create the gradient to go from the spot color to a 0% tint of the same spot color (for example, go from red to 0% red). That way, when you do your seps, the entire gradient will appear on the red separation.

   ## CORRECT IN CMYK OR RGB?

We've been asked the question of whether to correct in CMYK or RGB a hundred times. As a general rule, we try to do as much color correction as possible in RGB mode, and if we're going to use the image on press, we only convert to CMYK at the end of the correction process. The main reason is that CMYK mode throws away data—a lot of data—and why would you want to correct an image with significantly less data than your scanner can capture? We want as much data as possible while correcting images, and when we're done, then we'll convert to CMYK and toss the data that won't be used on press.

STRAIGHTENING SCANS IN 10 SECONDS (OR LESS)

If you've scanned an image and it's crooked when you bring it into Photoshop, you can fix it in about 10 seconds flat. Just switch to the Measure tool (it lives behind the Eyedropper tool in the Toolbox) and drag it along the top edge of the image you want to straighten. That's the hard part (and that should give you an idea of how easy this technique is). Next, go under the Image menu, under Rotate Canvas, and choose Arbitrary. Photoshop automatically enters the amount of rotation (courtesy of your earlier measurement), so all you have to do is click OK and bam!—the image is perfectly straightened.

STAY AWAY FROM THE SPONGE TOOL

If you're creating images that will be output on a printing press, you're probably already familiar with gamut problems (colors that are so vivid and saturated that they're out of the range of CMYK printing). There's a tool in Photoshop called the Sponge tool that lets you paint over highly saturated areas to bring them back into gamut. Yup, it's there all right; we just don't recommend using it, because it does a somewhat harsh job of what Photoshop's going to do anyway when you convert the entire image to CMYK mode. Since Photoshop's going to do it anyway, why waste your time (and possibly mess up your image)?

REMOVING NOISE IN DIGITAL CAMERA IMAGES

If you shoot images with a digital camera, you can almost bet that the images (when opened in Photoshop) will have some unwanted noise. Most of this noise appears only within the Blue channel, and knowing that, you can go to the Blue channel and add a slight blur to just that channel. This helps get rid of the noise and leaves the detail in the other channels untouched. Here's how:

1. Open your digital camera image in Photoshop.

2. Go to the Channels palette and click on the Blue channel to make it active.

3. Go under the Filter menu, under Blur, and choose Gaussian Blur. When the Gaussian Blur dialog appears, add a slight bit of blur (we can't give you a specific value; you'll have to experiment, but start at 0.5 and move slowly upward using the Up Arrow key on your keyboard).

4. When the noise has pretty much disappeared, click on the RGB composite channel and continue with your regular image correction.

SCANNERS AREN'T JUST FOR FLAT OBJECTS

Even though your flatbed scanner is normally used for scanning (you guessed it) flat images, it doesn't mean you can't scan images that have more dimension (such as a watch, a ring, a yo-yo, you name it). The only problem is, scanning an image that lifts the lid adds lots of ambient light into your scan, introducing so many outside colors and reflections that it makes the scan all but unusable. The tip for getting around this is deceivingly simple: Just put a black sweater (or black felt cloth) around the object you're going to scan, and you'll get great-looking scans, even with the lid open. The black sweater soaks up that ambient light and you'll be amazed at how natural and balanced your scanned objects will look.

REMOVING RED EYE WITH THE COLOR REPLACE BRUSH

Although this doesn't sound like a standard use for the Color Replacement tool, it works amazingly well for removing red eye from photos. Just press the letter "d" to set your Foreground color to black, grab the Color Replacement tool (it's under the Healing Brush in the Toolbox), click on the red area in one of the eyes, and then just paint it away (the brush will snap to the red color, which makes the repair a breeze). If this sounds like a weird use for the Color Replacement tool, it's not as weird as you think—just move your cursor over the tool's icon in the Toolbox, and you'll see the eye next to the icon turns red. Coincidence? I think not.

ARE YOUR COLORS PRESS READY?

If you're working on an image that will be printed on a printing press and you select a color that's outside the range of what a CMYK press can reproduce, you'll get what's called a Gamut Warning right within Photoshop's Color Picker. This is just to let you know that the color you've chosen is outside the CMYK gamut. Just below the warning (shown at left) is a tiny Color Swatch showing you what the color you picked will really look like when printed in CMYK mode. To find out where that color resides within the Color Picker, click once directly on that tiny swatch and Photoshop will pick that color for you.

NEVER SWAP COLORS AGAIN WHEN CLEANING LINE ART

When cleaning up line art images with the Pencil tool, you can spend a lot of time going back and forth to the Toolbox to switch your Foreground color to black (to fill in missing pixels) and then to white (to erase pixels that shouldn't be there in the first place). It does help if you use the keyboard shortcut "d" to set your Foreground to black, and then "x" to make your Foreground color white, but there's actually a faster way. Once you select the Pencil tool, go up in the Options Bar and turn on Auto Erase. What the Auto Erase option does is pretty neat—when you click the Pencil in a black area of pixels, it paints white; when you click it on a white pixel, it automatically paints black. It happens automatically—so you never have to switch colors again—saving you a ton of time, travel, and keystrokes.

LET PHOTOSHOP DO YOUR RESOLUTION MATH

You don't need a calculator to determine how much resolution you need for printing to a particular line screen—Photoshop will do all the math for you, right inside the Image Size dialog. Here's how: Open the image you want to print. Go under the Image menu and choose Image Size. When the dialog appears, click on the Auto button (it's right under the Cancel button). When the Auto Resolution dialog appears, all you have to do is type in the line screen of the device you're printing to and then choose a quality setting. Here's how Photoshop does its resolution math:

Draft: This just lowers your resolution to 72 ppi (ideal for onscreen use, the Web, etc.).
Good: This takes the line screen and multiplies it by 1.5.
Best: This doubles the line screen (multiplies it by 2).

When you click OK, Photoshop enters the resolution it just calculated into the Resolution field of the Image Size dialog.

GOING TO PRESS?
MAKE SURE YOUR MONITOR IS IN THE "RIGHT SPACE"

By default, the RGB space for your monitor is set to sRGB, which is an okay mode for designing Web graphics. However, if you're producing graphics for print, the sRGB mode is just about the worst RGB space your monitor could possibly be set at. It clips off lots of colors that are actually printable in CMYK mode, and therefore is pretty unsuitable for prepress work. We recommend changing your RGB workspace to an RGB space that's more appropriate for doing print work. We like Adobe RGB (1998), which is a very popular RGB space for prepress work. You choose this RGB space under the Photoshop menu, under Color Settings (in Windows, Color Settings can be found under the Edit menu). When the Color Settings dialog appears, under the Working Spaces areas, for RGB choose Adobe RGB (1998) from the pop-up list of working spaces.

WANT BETTER GRADIENTS ON PRESS? HERE'S THE TIP

If you're designing a job that will ultimately go to a printing press in CMYK mode and it's going to contain one or more gradients, you'll get better printed results (less color shifts) if you create those gradients after you convert to CMYK mode.

GETTING BEFORE AND AFTER PREVIEWS

If you're applying a correction filter, such as the Unsharp Mask filter, you can get a before and after view of your image even before you click the OK button (and then press Command-Z [PC: Control-Z] to undo/redo the filter). Instead, click-and-hold on the preview box inside the Unsharp Mask filter. When you click-and-hold, you get the before preview in the window; when you release the mouse button, it shows you how the image will look with the filter applied. Pretty handy. If you need to see the full preview on screen, you can toggle the Preview checkbox on or off. Another tip is to hold the Command or Option (PC: Control or Alt) button while in a filter dialog, and then your cursor changes into the Zoom tool. You can then zoom in or out in your preview window by clicking within it.

   CLONING FROM IMAGE TO IMAGE

If you're retouching an image using the Clone Stamp tool, not only can you clone from the image you're in but you can also clone from any other image that you have open. All you have to do is make sure both images are open at the same time. Go to the other image, Option-click (PC: Alt-click) on the area you want to clone from, switch back to the image you're working on, and then start painting. When you do, you'll be cloning image data from the other image.

GET MORE REALISTIC DROP SHADOWS ON PRESS

Here's a quick tip for getting more realistic drop shadows in print: Add some noise. In the Layer Style Drop Shadow dialog, there's a slider for adding noise to your shadows. When you add just a small percentage, it makes your shadows appear more realistic when they show up in print.

   MAKING SURE YOUR WHITES ARE REALLY WHITE

If you have an image that appears to have solid white areas (maybe the background surrounding a logo), but when you put the Eyedropper on that area, it gives you a 1% or 2% reading in one of the CMYK values in your Info palette, you can use Levels to gets those areas back down to 0% so they don't print with a dot. Here's how: Go under the Image menu, under Adjustments, and choose Levels. The third field from the left (at the top of the dialog) shows your current highlight value (your white point setting). The default value will be 255. Enter 252 or 250, then move your cursor over the white area in question and look in the Info palette to see if the readings are now all 0% (that change should be enough to remove the stray colors). When it's right, click OK, and you'll have solid white in your white areas.

TRY NOT TO CORRECT MORE THAN ONCE

When correcting images in Curves, Levels, etc., it's best to try and do all your corrections at one time rather than changing each setting individually (by that I mean, don't set a highlight in Curves, then close and reopen it to set a shadow). The reason is, each time you apply a tonal correction, it puts some strain on the quality of the image. So to keep your image from having unnecessary data loss, when you open Curves or Levels, make your shadow, highlight, and midtone adjustments, and then click OK to apply all three adjustments at once.

   HAVE PHOTOSHOP HELP FIND YOUR HIGHLIGHTS/SHADOWS

Not sure where the highlight or shadow points in your image are located? Let Photoshop help. Go under the Window menu and choose Show Info. In the RGB readout, click on the tiny Eyedropper icon to the left of the readout. A pop-up menu will appear with a list of values you can measure. Choose Total Ink from this pop-up list. Next, switch to the Eyedropper tool and move it over your image in the areas you think might be the darkest. Now, up in the Info palette, look for the highest number. When you find the area in your image with the highest number (the highest amount of total ink), you've found the shadow point. Do the same to find the highlight—just look for the lowest number. When you locate that number, you've found the highlight.

TALKIN' 'BOUT MY RESOLUTION

Here's a lingo tip about resolution. Although images can have a resolution from 1 to more than 2,000 ppi, when it comes to talking resolution, there are three basic resolutions that are pretty common. Low-res (short for resolution) is normally 72 ppi, and low-res images are primarily used for onscreen viewing (such as the Web, slide presentations, digital video, etc.). Medium-res is generally 150 ppi and is commonly used for printing to inkjet and laser printers. When people use the term high-res, it's almost always referring to 300 ppi, which is more than sufficient resolution for printing to a printing press. Anything above 300 ppi is still considered high-res, but you'd say it like this: "I made a 600-ppi high-res scan." Which resolution is right for you? Nice try. That's a whole book unto itself.

   ARE YOU REALLY SEEING YOUR SHARPENING?

When you apply sharpening to your image using the Unsharp Mask filter, make certain that when you apply it, you're viewing the image at 100% size. Most other views won't give you an accurate view of how the sharpening is really affecting the image. To make sure you're viewing at 100%, just double-click the Zoom tool in the Toolbox.

ADJUSTING CURVE POINTS WITH PRECISION

Once you've plotted a point on a curve, you can adjust these points by clicking and dragging them, but many people find it easier to plot the point by using the Up/Down Arrow keys on their keyboard. This adjusts the Output of the point in increments of 2. To adjust the Input, use the Left/Right Arrow keys. To make larger moves, hold the Shift key while using the Arrow keys and your points will move in increments of 15.

   ### APPLY UNSHARP MASK TO CMYK IMAGES

If you've already converted your image to CMYK mode and you want to quickly sharpen your image without introducing color shifts or halos, go to the Channels palette, click on the Black channel, and apply your Unsharp Mask there. Applying the filter just to the Black channel will enable you to apply a higher level of sharpening without damaging the image.

RGB FLESH TONES: GETTING THE "RED" OUT

If you're working on an RGB image and you've done your basic color correction but the flesh tone in your image still seems too red (a common problem), here's a tip to fix it fast. First, select the flesh tone areas in your image (using the Lasso tool, etc.). Add a slight feather by going under the Select menu and choosing Feather. Enter a 1-pixel feather for low-res images; 3-5 pixels for high-res images. Go under the Image menu, under Adjustments, and choose Hue/Saturation. From the Edit pop-up menu, choose Reds. Now lower the Saturation slider until your skin tones look more natural, and click OK.

   ONCE YOU'RE IN CMYK MODE, STAY THERE

You've read some techniques in this chapter that require you to be in either RGB mode or Lab Color mode; however, if for any reason your image is already in CMYK mode, do not (I repeat, do not) convert to RGB or Lab mode for *any* reason. Once you've converted to CMYK mode, the data loss from the conversion has already occurred, and switching back to RGB mode won't bring back those lost colors. What's worse is, if you switch from CMYK to RGB (or Lab), when you convert back to CMYK mode, you'll go through another CMYK conversion and damage your image even more. The moral of this story is—once you're in CMYK mode, stay there.

THE SIMPLE TIP TO BETTER COLOR SEPARATIONS

Converting from RGB mode to CMYK mode for printing is easy; just choose CMYK from the Mode menu under the Image menu. However, getting great-looking separations on press takes more than just choosing the CMYK menu command. Before you convert to CMYK mode, call the print shop that's printing your job and ask them for their Photoshop CMYK separation setup. They'll provide you with custom settings to input in the CMYK Setup dialog that will give you a separation that's tuned to their particular printing press. Once they provide you with those settings, you input them by going under the Photoshop menu and choosing Color Settings (in Windows, Color Settings can be found under the Edit menu). When the Color Settings dialog appears, click on the CMYK pop-up menu, and at the top of the menu choose Custom CMYK. The Custom CMYK setup dialog will appear, where you can enter the settings given to you by the print shop. Once entered, then you can make your CMYK conversion, and you'll get a better separation that's specially tuned to the press your job will be printed on.

   ## HOW TO SHARPEN FLESH TONES IN CMYK

When you're sharpening CMYK images, one of the toughest areas to sharpen are the flesh tones. Oftentimes, because of the soft nature of skin, you'll need a lot of sharpening, which can introduce noise and color shifts, particularly in flesh tone areas. One tip that's often used to combat this is to apply your sharpening to just the Cyan channel in the Channels palette in images where flesh tone is the focal point of the image (such as in portraits).

HOW TO READ FOUR AREAS AT ONCE

Photoshop's Color Sampler tool lets you sample up to four different color readings from within your image at the same time. The cool thing is, any time you have one of Photoshop's paint tools (Brush, Clone Stamp, Eraser, etc.), you can instantly access the Color Sampler by holding Shift-Option (PC: Shift-Alt). Click to add a Color Sampler and the Info palette immediately pops up to show you the reading. Each time you add a Sampler, the Info palette expands to show that reading (leaving your earlier readings still visible). To delete any Sampler, press Shift-Option (PC: Shift-Alt) again and just move the cursor back over the Sampler and it will change into a pair of scissors. Click right on the Sampler in your image to delete it (hint: you have to click directly on the sampler or it won't work).

MORE CURVE POINT QUICK TIPS

When you're working in Curves, once you've plotted a curve point, you can rotate over to the next point in your curve by pressing Control-Tab (PC: Right-click-Tab). To rotate back to the previous point, add the Shift key to make it Shift-Control-Tab (PC: Shift–Right-click–Tab). If you've got one or more points selected and want to deselect all your points, just press Command-D (PC: Control-D) to release all your points.

Speed Kills

ADVANCED
TIPS

Before you attempt any of the tips in this chapter, I have to tell you, you'll need a fairly thorough knowledge of calculus, and it wouldn't hurt if you kept

Speed Kills

advanced tips

a scientific calculator handy either. In fact, ideally, you'd put together a team with varied backgrounds and skill sets to really get anything out of this chapter. Believe it or not, that's what some people expect from an advanced tips section—tips that are very complicated and involved. But just because you're a more advanced user doesn't mean the tips should be harder; it just means the tips apply to more advanced areas of Photoshop use, such as Masking, Curves, Paths, and fun stuff like that.

The tips should be easy to do, just covering more advanced topics. But if you really feel you need a complicated and involved tip to get your money's worth, here goes: Open a blank RGB document at 72 ppi. Then take a photograph of your family and tape it to the outside of your monitor. Using the Airbrush tool, choose a large soft-edged brush, and draw what you see. When complete, it should look exactly like the photograph. Happy now?

USING THE FILE BROWSER TO OPEN 16-BIT IMAGES

While it may be obvious that you can open 16-bit images from the Open menu, many people don't realize that you can now open Raw images from right within the File Browser. In fact, it treats 16-bit Raw images just like any other image—just double-click to open it. When you double-click, the File Browser launches the Camera Raw plug-in so you can process your Raw image before it's opened in Photoshop.

KEEPING TRACK OF YOUR EVERY MOVE

If you'd like to keep a running record of every step, every tweak, every movement—virtually every little thing you've done to your image, in Photoshop CS—you can do just that. It's called History Logging. Basically, it keeps a running log (in the background) of all your History States, and it can save it to a text file that you can open and view later. To turn on this History Log, go under the Photoshop menu (PC: Edit menu), under Preferences, and choose General. At the bottom of the General Preferences dialog, turn on the checkbox for History Log, then choose if you want the log items embedded into the file (metadata), written to a text file, or both.

EMBED YOUR MESSAGE INTO YOUR PHOTOS

As you know, your digital camera embeds background info into your photos (called EXIF data) and Photoshop embeds its own info when you edit the image (called File Properties). However, in Photoshop CS you can add your own info (called IPTC data) in the IPTC area within the Metadata palette in the File Browser. This is where you might embed your copyright info, Web site, or other comments that people viewing your file might find important. To add your info, just click to the right of any IPTC item that has a Pencil icon in front of it, and a field will appear where you can enter your own custom info.

   MANAGING THE METADATA OVERLOAD

The Metadata palette provides much more information than the average person will ever need. If you don't need all this "metadata overload," you can set it up so it only displays the data you care about, giving you a more orderly, easier-to-read Metadata palette. To do this, go to the Metadata tab, click on the right-facing triangle button to the right of the tab, and from the pop-down menu, choose Metadata Display Options. In the dialog that appears, uncheck any fields you don't need displayed, turn on the Checkbox at the bottom for Hide Empty Fields, and click OK.

PHOTOSHOP'S OWN SLIDE SHOW

If you don't want to create a full PDF Presentation, you can create a mini slide show right within Photoshop itself. Just open all the images you want in your slide show, then Shift-click on the Full Screen Mode icon near the bottom of the Toolbox (it's the third icon from the left), then press the Tab key on your keyboard. To step through your slide show, press Control-Tab.

THE HISTOGRAM PALETTE'S VISUAL CUES

When you're using Photoshop CS's Histogram palette, not only can you see a histogram of each individual channel (select the All Channels View option from the Histogram palette's pop-down menu) but you can use color as your visual cue to quickly see which channel is which. Just choose Show Channels in Color from the palette's pop-down menu, and then the Red channel histogram will appear in Red, the Green in green, etc.

SEEING YOUR FULL-COLOR IMAGE WHILE EDITING A CHANNEL

When you're working on an individual channel in the Channels palette, by default Photoshop displays your current channel onscreen in grayscale. If you make changes to that channel, you only see how the change affects that channel. However, there is a little-known trick that lets you see the full-color image, while editing the currently selected channel. While you're editing the channel, just press the Tilde key (~), which is right above the Tab key on your keyboard, and you'll see the full RGB preview as you edit.

   HOW TO COMBINE TWO PATHS INTO ONE

If you're using the Pen tool, and you've created multiple paths within your document, these paths are totally

separate, and are moved independently of one another. However, if you want these paths to move as one unit—combine them. Just switch to the Path Selection tool, then go up to the Options Bar and click on the Combine button. Now when you move one path, all the combined paths move right along with it.

POWER UP YOUR LAYER STYLES

Here's a little-known tip for controlling the intensity of your Layers Styles. This is particularly helpful if you've applied a number of different Layer Styles to a layer, and want to affect them all at the same time, rather than tweaking each one individually. It's called "Scale Effects," and it's buried in the Layer menu, at the bottom of the Layer Style submenu. Choose it, and a dialog appears with a slider set to 100% by default. As you increase the amount (up to 1000% maximum), it increases the "scale" of all your effects. For example, if you increased the scale of a Layer Style drop shadow, the shadow would become blurrier and its distance from the object would become greater. If you adjusted a Stroke Layer Style, the stroke would become thicker, etc. Pretty powerful stuff.

SWAPPING FILES? MAKE SURE YOUR COLOR STAYS INTACT

If you wind up sharing images you've created in Photoshop CS with anyone using an earlier version of Photoshop (such as Photoshop 4.0 or 5.0, both of which had different color-management setups, or in the case of 4.0, didn't really have one at all), your images will almost undoubtedly look different on their monitor than the same image does on your color-managed monitor.

The trick to getting around that problem is to change the color mode of your image to Lab Color *before* you save the file that you'll be giving to them. That way, they'll see your image in Lab Color mode without having your color management info embedded within the image. In short, their image will look much closer to your image.

FREEFORM/PEN TOOL QUICK SWITCH

If you're using the Freeform Pen tool, there are times when you may want to temporarily switch to the regular Pen tool so you can draw a straight line segment. You can actually do this by holding the Option key (PC: Alt key) and then releasing the mouse button. This temporarily switches you to the regular Pen tool so you can draw your straight line segment by moving the mouse. When you're done, click-and-hold, release Option/Alt, and you're back to the Freeform Pen tool.

VISUAL CONTROL OVER YOUR SELECTIONS USING QUICK MASK

Did you know that you can use Quick Mask mode to expand or contract your selections visually? Here's how: Create a selection (using any of Photoshop's selection tools), and then switch to Quick Mask mode (press the letter "q"). Now you can go to the Levels dialog and tweak the size of your selection. Moving the Midtone Input Levels slider to the far left makes the selected area smaller (contracting the selection). Moving the Midtone Input Levels slider to the far right makes the selected area larger (expanding the selection). The changes here usually aren't drastic, so you'd use this technique when a small adjustment to your selection is necessary, but seeing it like this beats the heck out of guessing.

BETTER COLOR-TO-GRAYSCALE USING LAB

Converting a color image to grayscale by choosing Grayscale from the Mode menu often produces some pretty flat-looking grayscale images. Rather than doing that, try one of our favorite tips for getting better grayscale images. Start with an RGB color scan, then go under the Image menu, under Mode, and choose Lab Color. Then go to the Channels palette. You'll see four channels. Drag the B channel to the Trash icon to delete it. Now, delete the channel called Alpha 2, leaving just Alpha 1 (which was the original Lightness channel). Now go under the Image menu, under Mode, and choose Grayscale. Go to the Layers palette and click on the Background layer. If your grayscale image appears too light, make a copy of the layer and change the Blend Mode to Multiply. If it appears too dark, lower your Multiply layer's Opacity until you dial in a perfect-looking grayscale image.

   HAVE PHOTOSHOP SELECT THE SHADOWS AND HIGHLIGHTS

This is a trick we use for prepress and for photo retouching because it instantly lets you select all the shadow areas (or highlight areas if you wish) for a particular image, and it's so easy because Photoshop does all the work. To have Photoshop select just the shadow areas in your image, go under the Select menu and choose Color Range. When the dialog appears, in the Select pop-up menu, choose Shadows, and click OK. The Shadow areas are instantly selected. This is ideal for situations where your scanner has plugged up the detail in the shadow areas (pretty common in most sub-$1,000 desktop scanners). Once the shadows are selected, you can "open them up" by going to Levels and moving the Midtone Input Levels slider to the left to bring back some of the shadow detail lost in the scan.

TROUBLESHOOTING ACTIONS? SLOW DOWN!

If you're an advanced user, chances are you're no stranger to using actions, and in fact, you probably create your own (rather than using the default actions that ship with Photoshop, many of which redefine the term "useless"). If you do create your own actions, you've already found that you spend more time troubleshooting your actions than you do creating them in the first place. Well, this little tip makes the troubleshooting process a lot easier, and saves you both time and frustration. The problem is (and this won't sound like a problem) Photoshop runs actions so quickly that you don't see each step, or each dialog, so tracking down a missing or wrong step is just about impossible. Luckily, you can actually slow down your action, or even put a pause between each step, by using Photoshop's Playback Options dialog found in the Actions palette's pop-down menu. When it appears, you can choose to play your action Step by Step, seeing everything as it happens, or you can choose to enter the number of seconds you'd like it to pause. Then, when you replay the action, you can see everything step by step and track down the culprit.

   ACCESSING GRAYED-OUT FILTERS IN CMYK

One of the bad things about converting from RGB mode to CMYK mode is that many of Photoshop's coolest filters can only be applied in RGB mode, and once you're in CMYK mode, many of them are "grayed out" in the Filter menu, so they can't be accessed. So what do you do if you really want to use one of those filters? (Whatever you do, don't convert back to RGB mode, then back to CMYK. That's image suicide.) Instead, try this tip: In the Channels palette, click on the Cyan channel. Go to the Filters menu and you'll notice that all those grayed-out filters are now suddenly available. All you have to do now is apply the filter you want to each channel individually (once each on Cyan, Magenta, Yellow, and finally the Black channel), and the filter will appear as though you applied it to the entire image (in reality, you did—you just did it the more laborious way). One way to speed up this process is to create an action that will do it all for you with one click of the mouse.

MORE CONTROL OVER FILTERS

We love Photoshop's Fade command (which acts like an "undo on a slider"), and when it comes to applying filters, we use it all the time to gain more control (including blending mode control) over filters we apply. The only downside to the Fade command is you can only use it one time—you get one opportunity to Fade, or choose a Blend Mode, then you're stuck. Here's a tip to keep the control of your filters for as long as you'd like: When you're about to apply a filter, make a duplicate of the layer where you're applying the filter, then apply it. This keeps the application of your filter fully editable—you can change Blend Modes as often as you like, change Opacity, add a Layer Mask to determine where the filter shows and where it doesn't, or even toss the layer in the Trash and start all over.

ASSIGNING METADATA TO MULTIPLE FILES

Want to assign metadata to more than one photo at a time? (Perhaps you want to embed your copyright info into 30 or more photos at once.) Just Command-click (PC: Control-click) on all the photos you want to affect, then enter the custom info you want (in one of the IPTC fields in the Metadata palette) and that info will be added to every selected photo at once.

APPLYING MULTIPLE FILTERS? NOT ON MY LAYER!

Thinking of applying a number of different filters to a particular layer? Don't do it. Instead, make a copy of your layer, then apply the first filter. Make another copy of the layer and apply the second filter; make another copy, apply the third filter, and so on. You can use Photoshop's Layer Blend Modes to get the effect that one filter is applied on top of the others, and now you've got full control over each individual filter applied. If you don't like one of the filters, just drag that layer into the Trash. Better yet, you've got Blend and Opacity control you wouldn't have by simply applying filter over filter.

   ## NEW SNAPSHOT, THE MISTAKE INSURANCE POLICY

The great thing about Photoshop's History feature is that you can (by default) undo your last 20 steps. Perhaps even more important is that you can always return to how the image looked when you opened it, so you never really do any permanent damage (as long as the file is open). However, what if you opened an image, worked on it for a while, and it was really looking great, but about 10 minutes later, it took a turn for the worse (this happens to us more often than we'd care to admit). If you undo the last 20 steps, it may not take you back far enough to the point that you want to return to, and the only other choice is to go all the way back to where you started. Here's a tip to keep you from pulling your hair out: Any time your image is at a stage where you think it looks pretty good, go to the History palette, and at the bottom of the palette, click on the New Snapshot button. Think of it as an insurance policy so that if things go bad, you can at least return to that spot and try again. It's not a bad idea to create a new Snapshot about every five minutes when you're working on a big project. To keep from loading up on snapshots, when you create a new one, delete one or two snapshots before it.

SAVING YOUR ACTIONS AS PRINTABLE TEXT FILES

This is a totally undocumented actions tip, and if you need it, it's a real lifesaver. Once you've created an action, you can actually save a text document with all the action steps so you can have a printed hard copy of your action. Here's how: In the Actions palette, click on the Action set containing the action that you want to save as a text document. Hold Option-Command (PC: Alt-Control) and from the Actions palette's pop-down menu, choose Save Actions. When the Save dialog appears, you'll notice that the three-letter file extension is .txt (indicating it's a text file) rather than .atn (which is the Photoshop action format). Click OK and you've got a text file you can open in any word processor to print out your steps.

   ## 3D PRINT EFFECTS (AND WHERE TO GET THOSE GOOFY GLASSES)

For a brief time back in the 1950s, 3D movies were all the rage, but it was short-lived, probably because you had to wear those cheesy-looking 3D glasses to experience the effect. Although 3D has come a long way since then, unfortunately you still have to wear the cheesy glasses. Be that as it may, the 3D effect is starting to appear again in print ads in trendy magazines, which generally include the paper 3D glasses in the magazine. This effect can be created in Photoshop, no problem. The hardest part is finding a supplier for 3D glasses (okay, we'll help on that part too. Try 3D Glasses Direct at www.3dglasses.net). Here's a tip on how to create the 3D effect in Photoshop: Open an RGB image, then go to the Channels palette and click on the Red channel. Go under the Filter menu, under Other, and choose Offset. For Horizontal enter –5 and leave Vertical set to zero. For Undefined Areas, choose Repeat Edge Pixels, then click OK. In the Channels palette, click on the RGB channel to reveal the effect. Then, lastly, you have to determine which part you want to appear as "coming out of the image" toward the person viewing it. Switch to the History Brush and using a soft-edged brush, paint over the area you want to "jump out" from the image. As you paint with the History Brush, you'll see your original untouched image paint back in (don't sweat it; that's what it's supposed to do). Now all you have to do is order the glasses.

CREATING REUSABLE DIAGONAL GUIDES

If you've used Photoshop's rulers at all, you know that you have your choice of either a vertical or horizontal guide. That's not a bad thing, but there's one thing missing—a diagonal guide. Since Photoshop doesn't have one, here's a tip for making your own: Start by creating a new layer, then set your Foreground to R=74, G=132, B=255 (the color Photoshop uses for its built-in guides). Switch to the Line tool found in the Shapes tools, and on this new layer draw a diagonal line where you want your guide to appear (make sure you have Create Filled Region selected in the Options Bar). It's not a bad idea to copy that layer into a separate document and save it on your drive—so any time you need a diagonal line, you can just open that document and drag it right in.

   LOCKING YOUR TABLET BRUSH SETTINGS

Since Photoshop 7, the one thing that drove Wacom tablet users insane was that you couldn't lock in your pressure sensitivity settings without saving a special custom brush. Luckily, that all changed in Photoshop CS, and you can now lock in your pressure settings. Go to the Brushes palette and choose Expanded View in its drop-down menu. Then, in the left column of brush options, you'll see a little lock icon to the right of each category. Turn on Pen Pressure (or any of the tablet settings from the pop-up menus) then click the lock icon, and as you change and tweak brushes, your Pen Pressure stays locked in.

THE SECRETS OF SEARCHING IN THE BROWSER

Don't get caught in the trap of
thinking that you have to assign
keywords to your photos before
you can start using the File Browser's Search function (although keywords certainly make it easier). But
to find out just how much power

the search function really has, just click on the binoculars icon in the Toolbar at the top of the
File Browser, then click-and-hold the first Criteria pop-up menu. If you remember you shot the
photo you're looking for with a certain camera, you can search the EXIF data for that make and
model. You can also search by Rank, whether it was flagged or not, and a host of other criteria.

   DRAG-AND-DROP CURVES FOR QUICK CORRECTION

If you're color-correcting a number of images that
are basically the same (for example, catalog shots or
high school yearbook shots, where the lighting and
composition are pretty much the same), you may
want to apply the same Curve setting to a number
of images. Rather than saving the Curve setting
and loading it each time, try this tip: Use a Curves
Adjustment layer, and then just drag-and-drop that
layer from your current image to your target image.

ACTIONS POWER TIP: ADD AN ACTION TO YOUR ACTION

Here's an Actions power tip: Did you know that you can build an action that will include an existing action? Here's how it's done: As you're recording your action, just go to the Actions palette, click on the existing action you want to include in your current action, and press the Play button at the bottom of the Actions palette. The existing action will now be added as a step in your current action (pretty scary stuff).

PREPRESS CLEANUPS—IN A SNAP

This is a great tip if you're zoomed in close to an image for retouching, or checking it in prepress for spots or specs, because it lets you check the entire image in a very methodical way—using your keyboard to navigate zone by zone. Here's how:

- Press the HOME key to jump to the upper left corner of your image window.
- Press the END key to jump to the lower right corner of your image window.
- Press the PAGE UP key to scroll upward one full screen.
- Press the PAGE DOWN key to scroll downward one full screen.
- Press Command-PAGE UP (PC: Control-PAGE UP) to scroll one full screen to the left.
- Press Command-PAGE DOWN (PC: Control-PAGE DOWN) to scroll one full screen to the right.

Once you've learned these shortcuts, you can start by pressing the Home key (jumping you to the upper left-hand corner of your image). Clean that area then press the Page Down key to move methodically down the left side of your image until you reach the bottom of your window. Then press Command-Page Up (PC: Control-Page Down) to move one screen to the right, clean that area, then press the Page Up key to move methodically up the image until you reach the top. Repeat these steps until you're finished. The advantage of doing it this way, besides the sheer speed of using keyboard shortcuts, is that you'll see every area of the image without missing a spot.

BLEND MODE POWER TIP

Once you understand layer Blend Modes, you wind up using them all the time. Chances are by now you know which individual modes you want to use (such as Overlay, Multiply, Soft Light, Hard Light, Screen) and which ones you'll probably never use (such as Dissolve). If you know which ones you want to use, you can use a keyboard shortcut

to jump right to the Blend Mode you want. For example, to jump to the Overlay mode for a layer, press Shift-Option (PC: Shift-Alt) and the first letter of the mode you want, in this case, the letter "O" (making the shortcut Shift-Option-O [PC: Shift-Alt-O]). For Screen mode, you'd press Shift-Option-S (PC: Shift-Alt-S), and so on. (Note: If you have a tool selected that has a Blend Mode in its Options Bar, the keyboard shortcut will change that Blend Mode instead of the layer Blend Mode.)

   MAKING CHANGES TO RAW PHOTOS WITHOUT OPENING THEM

This is a pretty slick trick—editing Raw photos without actually opening them in Photoshop, well, technically. Here's how it's done: Open the Raw digital camera image from within the File Browser, and it brings up the Camera Raw dialog. Make the tonal processing changes you want within the Camera Raw interface, but DON'T click OK. Instead, hold the Option key (PC: Alt key) and you'll see the OK button change into an Update button. Click on it (when it says Update) and Camera Raw will close, without the photo opening in Photoshop, but the changes you made will be visibly applied to the thumbnail in the File Browser. (Note: Like all changes in the Browser, they will not be applied until you actually open the photo in Photoshop.)

NO MORE CREATING TYPE IN CHANNELS

If you've ever tried to create and format type in a Channel, you know what a pain it can be. Especially because, when you're working in a channel, it doesn't create an editable Type layer, so you're really limited as to how you can format and of course, edit your type. So instead of creating type in a channel (which many special channel-type effects call for), just create your type on a layer as usual. In fact, don't go to the Channels palette at all—just pretend you're not using channels. Once you've got your type formatted and adjusted just the way you want it on your regular Type layer, Command-click (PC: Control-click) on your Type layer's name in the Layers palette. This puts a selection around your type. Now you can go under the Select menu and choose Save Selection. When the dialog appears, click OK, and it saves your perfectly formatted type as (you guessed it) a channel. Now you can delete your Type layer, and you're left with an Alpha channel with perfectly formatted type.

   LET PHOTOSHOP TELL YOU THE HIGHLIGHT AND SHADOW

We use this tip to have Photoshop help us determine which are the darkest (shadow) points and which are the lightest (highlight) points in an image when we're color correcting. We start by choosing a Threshold Adjustment layer from the bottom of the Layers palette. When the Threshold dialog appears, we drag the slider all the way to the left and the image turns completely white. We then slowly drag the slider back to the right, and the first black pixels that appear on screen are the shadow areas. We make a mental note of that area as our shadow point. Then we drag the slider all the way to the far right (the image turns black). As we drag slowly back toward the left, the first white pixels that appear are the highlight points in the image. We note them as well. We now know where the shadow and highlight points are in the image, and we can use them, along with the Eyedropper tools in the Curves dialog, to set the proper shadow and highlight areas to remove any color casts. Note: When you've determined where the shadow and highlight areas are, you can then delete the Threshold Adjustment layer by dragging it into the Trash icon at the bottom of the Layers palette.

USING THE LASSO—DON'T STOP TO NAVIGATE

If you're using the Lasso tool, you have a surprising amount of navigation control, even while you're dragging out your selection. For example, if you're drawing a selection and you need to scroll over a bit, just press-and-hold the Spacebar, and right where your cursor is, the Hand tool will appear and you can move the image while you're still selecting (try it once and you'll see what we mean). When you let go of the Spacebar, you're right where you left off, and you can continue your selection. Here's another Lasso tip: If you're drawing a selection and reach the edge of your document window and need to scroll over, hold the Option key (PC: Alt key), let go of the mouse button, move your mouse to the edge of your image window, and you can nudge the screen over (again, this is one you have to try once to understand it). It's like you're using the Lasso tool to slide the image over. When you're done sliding, press the mouse button and release Option/Alt to continue selecting. Incidentally, while selecting, you can also use the Command- + (plus) and Command- – (minus) zoom in/zoom out tricks (PC: Control- + and Control- –).

   ## LOAD ANY SAVED SELECTION WITHOUT THE CHANNELS PALETTE

If you're working on an RGB image and you've saved a selection (by drawing a selection and choosing Save Selection from the Select menu), you can instantly reload that selection at any time, without going to the Channels palette. If you have only one saved selection, just press Option-Command-4 (PC: Alt-Control-4), and the selection will instantly appear onscreen. If you have a second saved selection, press Option-Command-5 (PC: Alt-Control-5), and so on. The key to remember is that the RGB channels take up the first three spots, so always start with 4 to load your first Alpha channel. Note: If you're working with CMYK images, remember to always start with 5, because the CMYK channels take up the first four spots.

PLOT MULTIPLE CURVE POINTS IN JUST ONE CLICK

Earlier in the book, we showed you how Photoshop will plot a point on the curve for you if you Command-click (PC: Control-click) on a color in your image you want plotted. However, there's a power tip that we waited until now to share—if you add the Shift key, making it Shift-Command-click (PC: Shift-Control-click), Photoshop will add a point for that spot on all the color channels for you. This works in both RGB and CMYK modes.

TOUGH SELECTION TIP

If you're struggling to make a selection of an image that's against either a background of a similar color or a very busy background, here's a masking tip to make the process easier: Add a Levels or Curves Adjustment layer above your image layer, and use it to dramatically increase the contrast in the image to help make the edges stand out. This will often help make the difference between the object's edge and the background more obvious. The great part is, you can totally damage the look of the image because you're using an Adjustment layer. When your selection is in place, just drag the Adjustment layer into the Trash icon to delete it, and your image is back to normal, but you've got that "impossible" selection still in place.

CHAPTER 10 • Advanced Tips   **215**

MAKING THE COLOR PICKER SHOW CMYK

If you're working in CMYK mode and you go to the Color Picker, it still displays RGB colors. This is a bit of a problem, because you think you're picking one color, but when you start to paint or fill with that color, you get the CMYK desaturated version. Here's a tip to get around that. When you're in CMYK mode and you go to the Color Picker, press Command-Y (PC: Control-Y), which is the shortcut for Proof Colors (found under the View menu). When you do this with the Color Picker open, it changes all the colors in the Color Picker to CMYK colors. That way, when you pick a color in the Color Picker, it looks the same when you paint or fill with it in your CMYK image.

   MOVING MULTIPLE CURVE POINTS AT ONCE

If you're working in the Curves dialog and you want to make more than one point active at the same time, click on one point (to make it active), then hold the Shift key and click on another. As long as the Shift key is held down, you can click on as many points as you'd like to make them active at the same time.

ADD TO YOUR SELECTIONS THROUGH THE CHANNELS PALETTE

If you've got the Channels palette open and you have multiple saved Alpha channels, you can load any Alpha channel as a selection by holding the Command key (PC: Control key) and clicking directly on the channel's name. This instantly loads the selection. An even better tip: If you hold the Command key (PC: Control key) then add the Shift key (making it Shift-Command/Shift-Control) and click on another Alpha channel, it adds that to your current selection. You can keep adding more selections to your original selection until, well, until you run out of Alpha channels.

EMBEDDING PATHS INTO ACTIONS

If you're creating actions and you want your action to include a path that you've created, you can do that, but you have to draw your path first, before you record your action. Once you've drawn your path, and it comes to the part of your action that requires the path, go to the Action palette's pop-down menu and choose Insert Path and that path will be stored along with the action.

MEASURE TWICE, LOOK ONCE

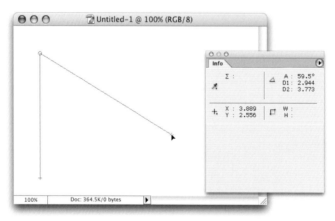

If you need to measure more than one side of an object (for example, if you're measuring a box, and you need both the height and width), you can measure both at the same time. First, open the Info palette (so you can see the measurements that the Measure tool generates), then get the Measure tool (under the Eyedropper) and click-and-drag it along the first edge. Release the mouse when you reach the end of the edge. Then hold the Option key (PC: Alt key), click on the end of the first line, and continue on in a different direction. You'll notice that another measurement line appears. Now, look up in the Info palette and you'll see your two measurements listed under D1 and D2.

STROKING HALF A PATH—HALF A PATH????

This is a mind-blowing advanced tip (not because it's hard—it's simple—but if you use the Pen tool, warning—your mind is about to spontaneously combust). Here's the scoop: If you're an advanced user, you already know that you can draw a path and then apply a stroke along that path (using the paint tool of your choice) by choosing Stroke Path from the Paths palette's pop-down menu. But dig this: If you draw your path, but only want to stroke a portion of that path, all you have to do is make a selection (using the Lasso tool) of the part of the path you want stroked. Then when you choose Stroke Path, it will only stroke the area of your path that is contained within your selection. Boom! That was the sound of our heads exploding.

SPEEDING UP BATCH ACTIONS

If you're running a Batch action on a folder full of images, one of the things that can really slow the process down is the fact that the History palette keeps creating History States (undos) for each image. To keep your Batch actions running at full speed, there are two things you can do: In the History palette's pop-down menu, under History Options, turn off the checkbox for "Automatically Create First Snapshot." Secondly, go under the Photoshop menu, under Preferences, and choose General (in Windows, Preferences can be found under the Edit menu). In the History States field, lower the number from 20 (the default) to 2 states and click OK. Then your batch will run like a greased pig. Don't forget to increase your History States or change your History Options back after you're done batching or you'll be down to two undos.

LOCKING A PDF PRESENTATION

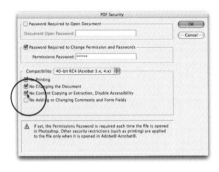

If you're using Photoshop to create a PDF Presentation slide show (under the File Browser's Automate menu) so you can e-mail it to your clients for proofing, one of your concerns may be that your client will just print your photos out to a photo-quality printer, leaving you out in the cold (so to speak). But you can pull the plug on their printing aspirations. When saving your PDF Presentation, under Output Options, choose Presentation, then hit Save. It'll ask you to name your PDF presentation (you're not done yet), so name it and click Save. When you name it and click Save, a PDF Options dialog will appear. Click on the PDF Security checkbox, then click on the Security Settings button. In the PDF Security dialog, click on the checkbox for Password Required to Change Permission and Passwords and enter (and memorize) a password. Then, under Compatibility, turn on the checkboxes for No Printing, No Changing the Document, and No Content Copying or Extraction, Disable Accessibility. Click OK and it'll ask for your password one more time. Now, when you e-mail the PDF Presentation, printing will be grayed out, and even if they have the full version of Acrobat, they won't be able to copy and paste your photos into something else for printing.

   SAVING TIME WHEN CORRECTING CAMERA RAW PHOTOS

If you're shooting and correcting Raw images from your digital camera, there's a File Browser trick you can use to quickly correct photos taken in similar lighting conditions. First, open the File Browser, then double-click on your first Raw image. This opens Camera Raw. Make your adjustments, then click OK in Camera Raw. This will open the image in Photoshop, but go back to the File Browser for now. Command-click (PC: Control-click) on the other Raw thumbnails in the File Browser that have similar lighting conditions. Once all the photos are selected, go under the Automate

menu and choose Apply Camera Raw Settings. In the resulting dialog, the Apply Settings From pop-up menu should be set to First Selected Image. Click Update and you'll see the thumbnail previews update to reflect your correction (which will be applied automatically when you open these images in Photoshop).

PUTTING YOUR LENS FLARE ON THE SPOT

This tip lets you precisely position the center of the Lens Flare filter by using the Info palette and a little-known feature of the Lens Flare dialog. First, open the Info palette (found under the Window menu) then put your cursor over the precise spot in your image where you'd like the center of your Lens Flare to appear. Then look up in the Info palette, under the X and Y coordinates, and write down those two coordinates (I knew one day I'd find a use for the X and Y coordinate readings). Then go under the Filter menu, under Render, and choose Lens Flare. There's a fairly large preview window in the center of the dialog. Hold the Option key (PC: Alt key), click once on the Preview window, and it brings up the Precise Flare Center dialog. Enter those X and Y coordinates you wrote down earlier (you did write them down, right?), click OK, and your Lens Flare is precisely positioned.

Index

Symbols

3D print effects, 208
3D Transform filter, 48
16-bit images, 198

A

About Photoshop
    command, 81
actions
    adding to existing
        actions, 211
    batch, 219
    embedding paths into, 217
    playback of, 205
    problems with, 171
    recording, 211
    saving as text files, 208
    slowing down, 205
    text, 97
    troubleshooting, 205
    from Web sites, 171
Actions palette, 115, 171,
    211, 217
Add Anchor Point tool, 20
Add Noise command, 178
Adjustment layers, 70, 215
Adobe Photoshop. *See*
    Photoshop
Airbrush tool, 74
alignment, layers, 144
All Channels View option, 200
All Layers option, 100
Alpha channels, 217
animations, 114
Animations palette, 114
application switching, 169
arrowheads, 77
.atn extension, 171, 208
Auto Erase option, 185
Auto Resolution dialog, 185
Auto Select Layer feature, 168

B

background color, 59
Background Eraser tool, 85
Background layers
    copying, 75
    copying contents of, 143
    deleting, 111
    locking/unlocking, 75, 160
    missing, 136
    renaming, 139
    sharpening images, 180
    styles, 139
    unable to find, 164
backgrounds
    black, 82, 124
    blurring, 119
    seamless, 117
    tiled, 117
    transparent, 111
backscreening, 122
banding, 178
barrel distortion, 170
batch actions, 219
batch conversions, 115
batch ranking, 51
Batch Rename dialog, 34
Bitmap mode, 180
black-and-white images, 180
black backgrounds, 124
Blend Modes, 67, 137, 140, 212
Blue channel, 183
Blur filters, 70, 79, 123, 179
blurring
    backgrounds, 119
    depth of field and, 123
    Despeckle command, 179
    Gaussian Blur filter, 70,
        79, 179
    JPEG images, 119
    shadows, 125
bold text, 105, 160
bounding boxes, 69, 95

brightness, 118
browsers, 112
Brush Picker, 12, 81
Brush Sample, 81, 177
brush strokes, 13
Brush tool, 158
brushes
    accessing, 30
    adding effects to, 39
    airbrush control, 74
    creating, 15
    custom, 78, 86, 175
    default settings, 86
    disappearing tips, 158
    editing effects, 39
    graphics tablets and, 209
    Healing Brush, 64, 175, 177
    History Brush, 124, 208
    photographic brush tips, 65
    preset, 30, 46, 78
    previewing, 73
    rearranging, 3
    removing, 12
    resizing, 9
    samples, 81, 177
    shape of, 175
    softness, 83
    Special Effect Brushes, 65
    switching between, 30
    temporary, 15, 81
    troubleshooting, 158
    undo feature, 22
Brushes palette, 39, 46, 65, 73

C

Camera Raw dialog, 212
Camera Raw images, 198,
    212, 220
Camera Raw plug-in, 198
Cancel button, 24
canvas color, 59

Canvas Size dialog, 59
Channel pop-up menu, 19
channels
Alpha, 217
Blue, 183
CMYK, 214
color, 200–201, 215
editing content on, 201
Lightness, 178
RGB, 214
selecting, 19
type in, 213
viewing, 200
Channels palette
accessing filters, 205
adding to selections
with, 217
channel display, 201
removing noise, 183
sharpening images, 178, 193
Unsharp Mask, 191
Character palette, 93, 99
characters, special, 93
checkerboard pattern, 39
Clear Brush Controls
command, 86
Clear Guides command, 14
clipboard, 169
Clipping Groups, 48
Clipping Masks, 48
clipping paths, 145
Clone Stamp tool, 187
cloned images, 187
CMYK channels, 214
CMYK color, 126
CMYK images, 193
CMYK inks, 161
CMYK mode
accessing filters in, 205
caution about switching
from, 192
color corrections, 181
Color Picker, 216
conversions, 192–193, 205
gradients and, 186
monitors and, 161, 186

printing and, 161, 182,
184, 186
sharpening images, 191
vs. RGB mode, 181, 192
CMYK Setup dialog, 193
collage, 66
color
accuracy of, 174
background, 59
banding, 178
canvas, 59
channels, 200–201, 215
CMYK. See CMYK mode
combining, 129
converting to grayscale, 204
copying, 50
correcting. See color
correction
defaults, 41
duotones, 122
fills, 42
focusing attention with, 124
foreground, 49, 98
GIF images, 116
hexidecimal codes, 114, 116
hue, 192
indexed, 116
inks, 161
Lab, 178, 192, 202, 204
layers, 146
matching, 126
"mismatch" warning, 52
monitors and, 161, 202
Pantone, 25, 126
press-ready, 184
previewing, 162
printing, 161
replacing, 174, 184
RGB. See RGB mode
sampled, 50, 117, 194, 204
saturation, 192
separations, 181, 193
shadows, 127
shared images and, 202
Similar command, 40
spot, 181

sRGB, 52, 186
swapping, 185
two-color vs. four-color, 122
type, 98
Web and, 112, 116
Web-safe, 112
Color Balance, 84
color correction
CMYK vs. RGB mode, 181
correcting single color, 84
Curves Adjustment layer
for, 210
default settings, 176
drag and drop feature, 210
flesh tones, 192
highlights, 174
multiple corrections, 189
multiple images, 210
color modes
CMYK. See CMYK mode
grayscale images and, 159,
180, 204
Lab Color, 178, 192, 202, 204
printing and, 161
RGB. See RGB mode
Color palette, 17
Color Picker
CMYK mode, 216
Color Wheel, 128
Gamut Warning, 184
Pantone colors, 25
replacing color, 174
RGB mode, 216
color ramp, 17
Color Range command, 16
Color Range dialog, 204
Color Replacement tool, 184
Color Sampler tool, 194
Color Stops, 66
Color Swatches, 25, 57, 98, 184
color wheel, 128
columns, 104
commands
About Photoshop, 81
Add Noise, 178
Clear Brush Controls, 86

Clear Guides, 14
Color Range, 16
Convert to Paragraph Text, 102
Create Layers, 144
Create Work Path, 95
Crop, 80
Define Brush Preset, 78
Despeckle, 179
Export Layers To Files, 135
Fade, 206
Feather, 123
Free Transform, 61, 131
Image Size, 113
Insert Path, 217
Load Selection, 55
Lock All Linked Layers, 137
Merge Visible, 80, 134, 154
New Set From Linked, 147
Paste Layer Style To Linked, 149
Purge All, 60
Rasterize Layer, 94, 97
Replace Color, 174
Rotate, 9
Save, 82
Save Actions, 208
Save for Web, 109, 111, 118
Save Selection, 55
Shadow/Highlight, 174, 176
Similar, 40
Timing, 87
timing, 87
Web Color, 116
Convert to Paragraph Text command, 102
copying items
    Background layers, 75, 143
    color, 50
    images, 58, 69
    Layer Masks, 150
    layers, 23, 75, 141, 143
copyright symbol, 93
Create Layers command, 144
Create New Snapshot icon, 69
Create Work Path command, 95

Crop command, 80
Crop snapping, 159
Crop tool, 16, 43, 75, 129, 159, 170
cropping. *See also* trimming
    images, 16, 43, 80
    photographs, 129
    snapping and, 159
    Web graphics, 109
cursors
    selection shortcuts and, 37
    Type cursor, 99
curve points, 191, 194, 215–216
curves
    adjusting, 191, 194
    drag-and-drop, 210
    magnified view of, 18
    reusing settings, 15
Curves Adjustment layer, 210
Curves dialog, 8, 18, 194, 216
Custom CMYK dialog, 193
Custom Color Picker, 25
Custom Shape tool, 93
Custom Thumbnail Size, 71, 86
customizing
    brushes, 78, 86, 175
    highlights, 176
    shadows, 127, 176
    shapes, 93
    styles, 113
    views, 71
cyan kicker, 124

D
Define Brush Preset command, 78
Delete Anchor Point tool, 20
deleting items
    filters, 28
    layers, 53, 111
    points, 10
    preferences, 163, 168
depth of field, 123
design tips, 121–131
Despeckle command, 179
diagonal guides, 209

digital cameras
    EXIF data, 199
    image resolution, 158
    importing images, 158
    Raw images, 198, 212, 220
    removing noise from images, 183
    sRGB color and, 52
Display and Cursors preferences, 158
distortion, 170
docking, 43
Document Bounds option, 159
documents. *See* files
drag and drop feature
    color correction, 210
    Curves Adjustment layer, 210
    folders, 68
    images, 78
    layers, 138, 141–142
    styles, 138
drawing lines, 209
Drop Shadow option, 125, 127
drop shadows
    adding noise to, 188
    angle adjustments, 142
    blurred, 125
    color, 127
    Global Light feature and, 165
    layers and, 142
    noise and, 188
    opacity, 125
    printing over solid colors, 167
    problems with, 165, 167
    softness, 125
    transparency, 125
dumb quotes, 92
duotones, 122
Duplicate Layer dialog, 141

E
Easter Eggs, 67
edge fringe, 66

editing
channel content, 201
on paths, 103
text, 99
type, 98, 103
effects
3D, 208
brush, 39
Filter Gallery, 27
layers, 145, 152, 202
modifying intensity, 68
print, 208
scaling, 202
undoing, 68
EPS files, 45, 162
EPS Options dialog, 162
erasing items, 85
EXIF data, 199
Export Clipboard option, 169
Export Layers To Files
command, 135
extensions
.atn, 171, 208
.psd, 170
.txt, 208
Extract function, 64
Eye icon, 138, 146
Eyedropper icon, 116
Eyedropper tool, 50, 111, 114,
117, 189

F

Fade command, 206
Fade dialog, 177–178
Feather command, 123
Feather field, 165
Feather Selection dialog, 79
feathered selections, 56, 79
feathering, 56, 79, 165
fields, escaping, 24
File Browser
closing, 11
Custom Thumbnail Size, 71
docking and, 43
Full Screen Mode, 59, 71
jumping to folders, 68

nesting palettes, 29
opening 16-bit images, 198
previews and, 41
refreshing, 38
saving folders in, 29
saving setups, 2
searching in, 210
side-by-side previews, 86
thumbnails, 86
File Handling preferences, 112
files
assigning metadata to, 206
batch renaming, 34
closing, 60
converting layers to, 135
EPS, 45, 162
finding, 210
finding exact center, 4
flagged, 72
GIF, 108
JPEG, 115
layered, 135
presets, 4
recalling previous
settings, 18
recent, 50
saving changes, 60
sharing, 202
size of, 108–109, 119,
147, 170
text, 208
transparency and, 108
Fill dialog, 42, 55
fills
color, 42
shortcuts, 55
"un-filling" layers, 153
Filter Gallery
default settings, 3
deleting filters, 28
modifying settings, 26
showing effects in, 27
zooming in, 26, 28
filters
3D Transform, 48
accessing in CMYK
mode, 205

applying, 206
Blur, 70, 79, 123, 179
controlling, 206
deleting, 28
Gaussian Blur, 70, 79, 179
grayscale images and, 159
layers and, 67, 207
Lens Flare, 221
multiple, 207
Photo Filters, 70
reapplying previous, 40
RGB, 159
Unsharp Mask, 178, 190–191
Find and Replace Text
dialog, 104
finding items
files, 210
highlights, 189, 213
items in File Browser, 210
layers, 164
palettes, 10
photos, 210
shadows, 189, 213
text, 104
Flagged Files feature, 72
flattening layers, 80, 134, 170
flesh tones, 192–193
floating selections, 151
folders
dragging, 68
jumping to, 68
plug-ins, 161
saving in File Browser, 29
Web images, 115
fonts. See also text; type
changing, 97
changing size, 99
converting to paths, 126
converting to
selections, 126
metadata, 35
foreground color, 49, 98
Foreground Color Swatch, 98
formats
GIF, 108–109
JPEG, 109, 162
TIFF, 167

Free Transform bounding
box, 164
Free Transform command,
61, 131
Free Transform handles, 61
Free Transform tool, 77, 170
Freeform Pen options, 166
Freeform Pen tool, 203
Full Screen Mode, 6, 59, 71

G

gamut problems, 182, 184
Gamut Warning, 184
Gaussian Blur filter, 70, 79, 179
ghosting, 122
GIF files, 108
GIF format, 108–109
GIF images, 116
Global Light feature, 165
gradient banding, 178
Gradient Picker, 21
gradients
    CMYK mode and, 186
    color separations, 181
    Color Stops, 66
    prepress work and, 186
    spot color, 181
graphic elements. See also
    images
    cropping, 109
    isolating, 122
    overlapping, 123
    for Web, 109, 113, 118
graphics tablet, 177, 209
grayscale images, 159, 204
Grayscale mode, 159, 180, 204
grids, 8
guides
    diagonal, 209
    flipping, 14
    slicing images at, 110

H

Hand tool, 57, 71, 214
handles, Free Transform, 61

Healing Brush tool, 64, 175, 177
hexidecimal codes, 114, 116
hiding layers, 138
High Pass dialog, 180
highlighting text, 94
highlights. See also light
    correcting, 174
    customizing, 176
    default settings, 176
    finding, 189, 213
    selecting, 204
Histogram palette
    display options, 200
    refreshing, 35
History Brush, 22, 124, 208
History feature, 207
History Logging, 198
History Options, 219
History palette
    batch actions, 219
    focusing attention with
        color, 124
    snapshots, 69, 207
    undo feature, 20, 76
History States, 219
horizontal guides, 209
HSV Picker, 128
HTML code, 114
HTML editor, 114
hue, 192
Hue/Saturation dialog, 192

I

Ignore Palettes option, 76
image correction, 173–185
Image Previews feature, 112
Image Size command, 113
Image Size dialog, 113, 185
ImageReady, 110–111
    styles and, 113
    Tile Maker, 117
    Web animations, 114
images. See also graphic
    elements; photographs
    16-bit, 198
    before and after views, 187

batch converting for
    Web, 115
black-and-white, 180
Camera Raw, 198, 212, 220
centering with black
    background, 82
changing placement of, 71
cloning, 187
CMYK, 193
copying, 58, 69
cropping, 16, 43, 80
dragging, 78
fitting to screen, 49
flagged, 72
grayscale, 159, 204
importing, 158
JPEG, 119
line art, 180, 185
moving with Hand tool, 71
navigating between, 13
noise in, 183
numbers in corner of, 108
opening, 11
optimized, 111
overlapping over text, 123
pasting, 58
previewing, 112
ranking, 51, 72
Raw, 198, 212, 220
resizing, 74
resolution. See resolution
RGB, 161, 192
scaling, 61
scanned, 23, 179–180
shared, 202
sharpening, 178, 180,
    190, 193
sliced, 110, 118
tiled, 65
viewing at 100% size, 49, 113
Web. See Web images
importing images, 158
indexed color, 116
Info palette, 218, 221
ink colors, 161
inkjet printers, 161
Input Levels slider, 122

Insert Path command, 217
Internet. *See* Web
Intersect with Selection
    icon, 46
IPTC data, 199, 206
italic text, 105, 160

J

jaggies, 5
JPEG files, 115
JPEG format, 109, 162
JPEG images, 119

K

kerning, 100
keyboard
    navigation, 211
    text spacing, 100
keyboard shortcuts
    Animations palette, 114
    Blend Modes, 212
    cursor and, 37
    Fill dialog, 55
    Gaussian Blur filter, 70
    Layers palette, 149
    modifier keys, 37
    multiple undos, 76
    navigation, 211
    resizing images, 74
    selection, 37
Keyboard Shortcuts editor, 70

L

Lab Color mode, 178, 192,
    202, 204
Lasso tool
    drawing straight
        segments, 36
    feathering, 56
    jaggies and, 5
    navigation control with, 214
    Polygonal Lasso, 10
    tips for, 5, 214
Layer Blend Modes, 207

Layer Comps feature, 139
Layer Effects, 145
Layer Masks
    copying, 150
    viewing as Rubyliths, 151
    viewing separately, 151
Layer menu, 136
Layer Properties dialog, 146
layer sets, 147
Layer Style dialog, 125, 136,
    140, 142
Layer Style Drop Shadow
    dialog, 188
layered files, 135
layers
    activating, 143
    Adjustment, 70, 215
    aligning, 144
    background.
            See **Background layers**
    blank, 175
    Blend Modes, 137, 140
    centered, 142, 144
    color-coding, 146
    comparing layouts, 139
    converting to separate
        documents, 135
    converting type layers to
        image layers, 94
    copying, 23, 75, 141, 143
    Curves Adjustment, 210
    deleting, 53, 111
    dragging between
        documents, 138,
        141–142
    drop shadow angles, 142
    effects, 145, 202
    file size and, 147
    filters and, 67, 207
    finding, 164
    flattening, 80, 134, 170
    healing on, 175
    hidden, 134, 138
    jumping to, 134, 143,
        149, 168
    layer-based slices, 118
    linked, 137, 147, 149

    locking/unlocking, 75, 137,
        146, 160
    merging, 147
    moving, 149
    navigating, 134, 143, 149,
        168
    nudging pixels in, 47
    opacity, 140, 153–154
    painting and, 146
    problems with, 160, 164, 168
    removing active effects
        from, 152
    retouching and, 72
    rotating, 9
    selecting everything on, 150
    selecting objects on,
        150–151
    Shape, 25, 145
    slices, 118
    styles, 138–139, 142, 144,
        149, 152, 202
    switching between, 149
    tips for, 133–154
    transparency, 143, 153
    turning off checkerboard
        pattern, 39
    Type, 94, 101, 146
    "un-filling," 153
Layers palette, 136, 148–149
Lens Flare filter, 221
Levels dialog, 122, 188
light. *See also* highlights
    Global Light feature, 165
    shadows and, 130
light source, 130
Lightness channel, 178
line art, 180, 185
Line tool, 209
lines
    arrowheads, 77
    drawing, 209
linked layers, 137, 147, 149
Load Selection command, 55
Lock All Linked Layers
    command, 137
Lock Transparent Pixels
    feature, 49

locked layers, 75, 137, 146, 160
Luminosity mode, 178

M

Mac OS–based systems
  Color Picker, 128
  deleting Photoshop
    preferences, 163
  Web graphics, 118
Magic Wand tool, 16
Magnetic Pen tool, 166
Marquee snapping, 159
masks
  clipping, 48
  layer, 150–151
  Quick Mask mode, 203
  selections and, 203, 215
  Unsharp Mask filter, 178,
    190–191
Measure tool, 182, 218
measurement units, 34, 56,
    75, 218
memory
  clipboard, 169
  out-of-memory warnings, 22
  performance and, 169
  plug-ins and, 161
  problems with, 22, 162, 169
  purging, 60
  requirements for, 162
  undo feature and, 22
menus, hiding, 82
Merge Visible command, 80,
    134, 154
merging layers, 147
"Merlin Lives" Easter Egg, 67
messages
  Gamut Warning, 184
  "mismatch" warning, 52
  out-of-memory warnings, 22
  resetting warning
    dialogs, 44
metadata
  assigning to multiple
    files, 206

  assigning to photographs,
    199, 206
  display options, 199
  font sizes, 35
Metadata palette, 35, 199, 207
Midtone Input Levels slider,
    203–204
moiré patterns, 179
monitor
  brightness, 118
  CMYK mode and, 161, 186
  color accuracy, 161, 202
  prepress work and, 186
  shared images and, 202
Move tool, 27, 47, 99, 168

N

navigation
  between images, 13
  jumping to folders, 68
  jumping to layers, 134, 143,
    149, 168
  jumping to tools, 101
  keyboard, 211
  Lasso tool, 214
  layers, 134, 143, 149, 168
New dialog, 136
New Layer dialog, 160
**New Set From Linked
    command,** 147
New Snapshot button, 207
Ninness, Michael, 74, 82
noise
  adding to images, 178
  adding to shadows, 188
  digital camera images
    and, 183
  removing banding with, 178
  removing from images, 183

O

objects
  3D, 183
  finding center of, 14

  on layers, 150–151
  measuring, 218
  scanning, 183
  selecting, 150–151
  Step and Repeat
    function, 73
  transforming, 61
opacity
  healing process, 177
  layers, 140, 153–154
  shadows, 125
  sharpening and, 180
Opacity slider, 153, 177
Open button, 135
Open Recent menu, 50
optimization
  comparing image
    versions, 111
  graphics for Web, 115
  window speed and, 111
Options Bar, 21, 47

P

paint strokes, 13
painting
  layers and, 146
  pixels, 185
palettes
  Actions, 115, 171, 211, 217
  Animations, 114
  Brushes, 39, 46, 65, 73
  Channels. *See* **Channels
    palette**
  Character, 93, 99
  Color, 17
  default locations, 54
  docked, 52
  in File Browser, 29
  finding, 10
  hiding/showing, 7, 51
  Histogram, 35, 200
  History. *See* **History palette**
  Info, 218, 221
  Layers, 136, 148–149
  Metadata, 35, 199, 207

minimizing, 51
nesting, 29
Paths, 58, 219
Preview, 2
protecting, 76
saving, 82
snapping, 37
Swatches, 57
Web-safe Color, 112
zooming, 76
Pantone colors, 25, 126
Paragraph Text Size dialog, 104
Paste Layer Style To Linked command, 149
pasting items
images, 58
layer styles, 149
Patch tool, 64
Path Selection tool, 69
paths
combining, 201
converting fonts to, 126
editing type on, 103
embedding into actions, 217
hiding around shapes, 25
resizing, 69
selections and, 58
Stroke Path tool, 85, 219
stroking portion of, 219
text, 95
Paths palette, 58, 219
patterns
checkerboard, 39
moiré, 179
PDF Presentations, 200, 220
PDF Security dialog, 220
Pen tool
Auto Add/Delete option, 20
combining paths with, 201
Magnetic options, 166
path selection, 58
resizing paths, 69
switching to Freeform tool, 203
tips for, 20

Pencil tool, 185
performance, 169
Perspective feature, 170
Photo Filters, 70
photographic brush tips, 65
photographs. *See also* **images**
assigning metadata to, 199, 206
barrel distortion, 170
batch renaming, 34
comparing side-by-side, 86
cropping, 129
finding, 210
flagged, 72
flesh tones, 192–193
isolating elements on, 122
placing inside type, 96
ranking, 51, 72
Raw, 212
red eye, 184
retouching, 72
Photoshop
earlier versions of, 202
Easter Eggs, 67
History Logging, 198
IPTC data, 199
performance, 169
startup time, 161
pixels
feathered, 79
fixing stray, 16
moving selections by, 164
nudging, 47
painting, 185
removing edge fringe, 66
selecting on layers, 150
selection smoothing and, 16
transparent, 49
Playback Options dialog, 205
plug-ins
Camera Raw, 198
memory and, 161
trimming, 161
points
curve, 191, 194, 215–216
removing, 10
white, 188

Polygonal Lasso tool, 10
preferences
brush size, 158
deleting, 163, 168
Display and Cursors, 158
Export Clipboard, 169
File Handling, 112
Mac OS–based systems, 163
rebuilding, 168
recalling, 88
Windows-based systems, 163
Preferences dialog, 88
prepress cleanups, 211
prepress tips, 173, 186–194
presentations, 83, 200, 220
presets
brushes, 30, 46, 78
documents, 4
press-ready colors, 184
pressure sensitivity controls, 177, 209
Preview palette, 2
previews
before and after views, 187
brushes, 73
color, 162
EPS files and, 162
File Browser and, 41
RGB, 201
side-by-side, 86
thumbnails, 220
printers, 161
printing
3D print effects, 208
CMYK mode, 161, 182, 184, 186
color and, 161
color space and, 186
resolution, 158, 185
RGB mode, 161
text files, 208
production tips, 1–30
Proof Colors option, 216
.psd extension, 170
Purge All command, 60

Q

Quick Mask mode, 203
quotation marks, 92

R

RAM
clipboard, 169
out-of-memory
warnings, 22
performance and, 169
plug-ins and, 161
problems with, 22, 162, 169
purging, 60
requirements for, 162
undo feature and, 22
ranking images, 51, 72
Rasterize Layer command,
94, 97
rasterizing type, 97–98,
100, 131
Raw images, 198, 212, 220
Raw photographs, 212
Rectangular Marquee tool, 165
rectangular selections,
164–165
red eye, 184
rendering text, 94
Replace Color command, 174
Resample Image option, 158
Reset button, 24
resolution
digital camera images, 158
high, 190
images, 158
low, 190
medium, 190
printing images, 158, 185
printing presses and, 190
scanned images, 179–180
Web and, 190
retouching process, 72, 175
RGB channels, 214
RGB filters, 159
RGB images, 161, 192
RGB mode
color corrections, 181

Color Picker, 216
conversions, 192–193, 205
grayscale images, 159
"mismatch" warning, 52
printing and, 161
sharpening images, 178
vs. CMYK mode, 181, 192
RGB preview, 201
RGB space, 186
Rotate command, 9
rotation, layers, 9
Rubylith, 151
rulers, 56

S

saturation, 192
Saturation slider, 192
Save Actions command, 208
Save command, 82
Save for Web command, 109,
111, 118
Save Selection command, 55
saves, undoing, 82
saving
actions as text files, 208
changes to files, 60
File Browser setups, 2
folders, 29
palettes, 82
selections, 55
for Web, 109, 111, 118
Scale Layer Effects dialog, 202
scaling images, 61
scans
3D objects, 183
highlights and, 204
resolution, 179–180
shadows and, 204
straightening, 23, 182
screen cleanup, 7
scroll bars, 57
scrubbing, 42
scrubby sliders, 42
search feature
files, 210
highlights, 189, 213

items in File Browser, 210
layers, 164
palettes, 10
photos, 210
shadows, 189, 213
text, 104
selections
adding to with Channels
palette, 217
contracting, 203
converting fonts to, 126
expanding, 164, 203
feathered, 56, 79
floating, 151
intersecting, 46
Lasso tool, 214
layers, 150–151
loading, 214, 217
masking and, 203, 215
moving, 38
objects, 150–151
paths as, 58
Quick Mask mode and, 203
rectangular, 164–165
rounded corners, 164–165
saving, 55
shortcuts, 37
softening edges of, 56
tips for, 215
transforming, 61
separation, color, 181, 193
Shadow/Highlight command,
174, 176
shadows
adding noise to, 188
blurring, 125
color, 127
custom, 127, 176
decreasing, 176
default settings, 176
drop. See drop shadows
finding, 189, 213
length of, 130
light source and, 130
opacity of, 125
open, 174, 176

printing over solid
    colors, 167
problems with, 165, 167
selecting, 204
softening, 125
Shape layer, 25, 145
Shape Picker, 93
Shape tools, 25, 93, 145
shapes
    brush, 175
    converting text to, 126
    custom, 93
    hiding paths around, 25
sharpening images, 178, 180,
    190, 193
shortcuts
    Animations palette, 114
    Blend Modes, 212
    cursor and, 37
    Fill dialog, 55
    Gaussian Blur filter, 70
    Layers palette, 149
    modifier keys, 37
    multiple undos, 76
    navigation, 211
    resizing images, 74
    selection, 37
Show Channels in Color
    option, 200
Similar command, 40
Slice Options dialog, 118
Slice Select tool, 118
Slice tool, 108
sliced images, 110, 118
Slices From Guides feature, 110
slide shows, 83, 200, 220
sliders, 42, 68
smart quotes, 92
Snap To feature, 159
snapping
    cropped images and, 159
    palettes, 37
snapshots, 207
Spacebar, 57
spacing, text, 100, 104
special characters, 93

Special Effect Brushes, 65
spell checking, 103
Sponge tool, 182
spot color, 181
sRGB color space, 52, 186
startup time, 161
startup window, 44, 81
Step and Repeat function, 73
Stops, Color, 66
straight quotes, 92
straight segments, drawing, 36
Stroke Path tool, 85, 219
strokes
    brush, 13
    paint, 13
    paths, 85, 219
styles
    Background layers, 139
    custom, 113
    dragging and dropping, 138
    ImageReady and, 113
    layers, 138–139, 142, 144,
        149, 152, 202
Swatches palette, 57
symbols, 93

T

text. *See also* **fonts; type**
    actions, 97
    bold, 105, 160
    columns, 104
    converting shapes to, 126
    editing, 99
    faux styles for, 105, 160
    finding, 104
    highlighting, 94
    horizontal scaling, 102
    italic, 105, 160
    kerning, 100
    multiple adjustments to, 105
    overlapping images over,
        123
    rendering, 94
    replacing, 104
    spacing, 100, 104

spell checking, 103
vertical scaling, 102
warped, 160
wrapping, 102
text boxes, 95, 102
text files, 208
text paths, 95
Textured Image extraction, 64
Threshold Adjustment
    layer, 213
thumbnails
    Custom Thumbnail Size, 71
    File Browser, 86
    file size and, 112
    previews, 220
    Raw, 220
    size of, 71, 87
    turning off, 112
TIFF format, 167
Tile Maker, 117
tiled backgrounds, 117
tiled images, 65
Timing command, 87
tonal adjustments, 19–20
Tool Tips, 73
Toolbox
    hiding/showing, 45
    jumping to tools in, 101
tools
    Add Anchor Point, 20
    Airbrush, 74
    Background Eraser, 85
    Brush, 158
    Clone Stamp, 187
    Color Replacement, 184
    Color Sampler, 194
    Crop, 16, 43, 75, 129, 159, 170
    Custom Shape, 93
    default settings, 54
    Delete Anchor Point, 20
    Eyedropper, 50, 111, 114,
        117, 189
    Free Transform, 77, 170
    Freeform Pen, 203
    Hand, 57, 71, 214
    Healing Brush, 64, 175, 177
    jumping to, 101

Lasso. *See* **Lasso tool**
Line, 209
Magic Wand, 16
Magnetic Pen, 166
Measure, 182, 218
Move, 27, 47, 99, 168
Patch, 64
Path Selection, 69
Pen, 20, 58, 69, 166, 201, 203
Pencil, 185
Polygonal Lasso, 10
Rectangular Marquee, 165
rotating through, 53
Shape, 25, 93, 145
Slice, 108
Slice Select, 118
Sponge, 182
Stroke Path, 85, 219
Type, 94, 101, 126
Zoom, 36, 49, 76, 113
transformations
3D Transform filter, 48
Free Transform bounding
box, 164
Free Transform command,
61, 131
Free Transform handles, 61
Free Transform tool, 77, 170
objects, 61
selections, 61
transparency
backgrounds, 111
creating, 111
file size and, 108
layers, 143, 153
pixels, 49
Transparent option, 136
Trim dialog, 109
trimming. *See also* **cropping**
plug-ins, 161
Web graphics, 109
troubleshooting, 157–171
actions, 171, 205
banding, 178
barrel distortion, 170
brushes, 158
color printing, 161

Crop snapping, 159
deleting preferences,
163, 168
EPS previews, 162
faux styles, 160
gamut problems, 182, 184
grayscale images, 159
layer navigation, 168
memory problems, 22,
162, 169
"mismatch" warning, 52
moiré patterns, 179
performance, 169
print resolution, 158
rebuilding preferences, 168
resetting warning
dialogs, 44
selection problems,
164–165
shadows, 165, 167
slow startup, 161
Warped Text function, 160
.txt extension, 208
type. *See also* **fonts; text**
in channels, 213
in circular format, 92
color, 98
editing, 98, 103
moving, 99
on paths, 103
placing photos inside, 96
rasterizing, 97–98, 100, 131
resetting, 93
sharpness of, 114
for Web, 114
Type cursor, 99
Type layers, 94, 101, 146
Type tool, 94, 101, 126
typeface tips, 91–105

U

undo feature
brushes, 22
History Brush, 22
History palette, 20, 207
modifying effects, 68

multiple undo shortcut, 76
out-of-memory warnings
and, 22
undoing saves, 82
**Units & Rulers Preferences
dialog,** 56
Unsharp Mask filter, 178,
190–191
Use All Layers option, 72

V

vector EPS files, 45
vertical guides, 209
views, custom, 71

W

Wacom tablet, 177, 209
warning dialogs, 44
warnings
Gamut Warning, 184
"mismatch" warning, 52
out-of-memory
warnings, 22
resetting warning
dialogs, 44
warped text, 160
Web
actions from, 171
color and, 112, 116
image resolution and, 190
sliced images, 118
tips for, 107–119
type size and, 114
Web animations, 114
Web browsers, 112
Web Color command, 116
Web color values, 116
Web images. *See also* **images**
batch converting images
to, 115
cropping, 109
cross-platform issues, 118
sharpness of, 110
viewing at 100% size, 113
zooming and, 110

Web pages, 118
Web-safe Color palette, 112
Web-safe colors, 112
Welcome Screen, 44
white point setting, 188
windows
    rotating through, 111
    speed of, 111
    startup, 44, 81
    Welcome Screen, 44
    zooming, 76

Windows-based systems
    Color Picker, 128
    deleting Photoshop
        preferences, 163
    Web graphics, 118
wireless pens, 177

X

X coordinates, 221

Y

Y coordinates, 221

Z
Zoom field, 6
Zoom tool, 36, 49, 76, 113
zooming
    entering zoom
        percentages, 113
    Filter Gallery, 26, 28
    in/out, 36
    palettes, 76
    for sharper web images, 110
    tiled images, 65
    windows, 76

COLOPHON

The book was produced by the authors and their design team using all Macintosh computers, including a Power Mac G4 450-MHz, a Power Mac G4 500-MHz, a Power Mac G4 Dual Processor 1.25-MHz, a Power Mac G4 733-MHz, and Power Mac G4 933-MHz. We use Sony Artisan, LaCie Electron Blue 22 and Apple Studio Display monitors.

Page layout was done using Adobe InDesign 2.0. Our graphics server is a Power Mac G3, with two 60-GB LaCie external drives, and we burn our CDs to a TDK veloCD 24X CD-RW.

The headers for each technique are set in Adobe MyriadMM_565 SB 600 NO at 9.5 on 13 leading, with the Horizontal Scaling set to 95%. Body copy is set using Adobe MyriadMM_400 RG 600 NO at 9.5 points on 13 leading, with the Horizontal Scaling set to 95%.

Screen captures were made with Snapz Pro X and were placed and sized within Adobe InDesign 2.0. The book was output at 150 line screen, and all in-house printing was done using a Xerox Phaser 7700 DX.

PHOTOGRAPHY

Courtesy of Brand X Pictures

ILLUSTRATION

Scott Kelby
Felix Nelson

ADDITIONAL PHOTOSHOP RESOURCES

National Association of Photoshop Professionals (NAPP)
The industry trade association for Adobe® Photoshop® users and the world's leading resource for Photoshop training, education, and news.

http://www.photoshopuser.com

KW Computer Training Videos
Scott Kelby is featured in a series of Photoshop training videos and DVDs each on a particular Photoshop topic, available from KW Computer Training. Visit the Web site or call 813-433-5000 for orders or more information.

http://www.photoshopvideos.com

PlanetPhotoshop.com
"The Ultimate Photoshop Site" features Photoshop news, tutorials, reviews, and articles posted daily. The site also contains the Web's most up-to-date resource on other Photoshop-related Web sites and information.

http://www.planetphotoshop.com

Photoshop Down & Dirty Tricks
Scott is also author of the best-selling book *Photoshop CS Down & Dirty Tricks*, and the book's companion Web site has all the info on the book, which is available at bookstores around the country.

http://www.scottkelbybooks.com

Adobe Photoshop Seminar Tour
See Scott live at the Adobe Photoshop Seminar Tour, the nation's most popular Photoshop seminars. For upcoming tour dates and class schedules, visit the tour Web site.

http://www.photoshopseminars.com

Mac Design Magazine
"The Graphics Magazine for Macintosh Users" is a tutorial-based print magazine with how-to columns on Photoshop, Illustrator, InDesign, Dreamweaver, GoLive, Flash, and more. It's also packed with tips, tricks, and shortcuts for your favorite graphics applications.

http://www.macdesignonline.com

PhotoshopWorld
The convention for Adobe Photoshop users has now become the largest Photoshop-only event in the world. Scott Kelby is technical chair and education director for the event, as well as one of the instructors.

http://www.photoshopworld.com

Photoshop Hall of Fame
Created to honor and recognize those individuals whose contributions to the art and business of Adobe Photoshop have had a major impact on the application or the Photoshop community itself.

http://www.photoshophalloffame.com

ScottKelbyBooks.com
For information on Scott's other books, visit his book site. For background info on Scott, visit www.scottkelby.com.

http://www.scottkelbybooks.com

Adobe Photoshop CS Down
& Dirty Tricks
Scott Kelby
US$39.99, 0735713537

The Adobe Photoshop CS Book
for Digital Photographers
Scott Kelby
US$39.99, 0735714118

The Mac OS X Conversion Kit: 9
to 10 Side-by-Side, Panther Edition
Scott Kelby
US$29.99, 0735713898

The Photoshop Elements Book
for Digital Photographers
Scott Kelby
US$29.99, 0735713928

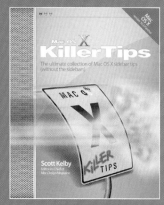

Mac OS X Panther Killer Tips
Scott Kelby
US$29.99, 0735713936

SCOTT
KELBY

Peachpit   New Riders